Mysteries of the Glory

UNVEILED

A New Wave of Signs and Wonders

by

David Herzog

Mysteries of the Glory Unveiled
Copyright © 2000 by David Herzog
ALL RIGHTS RESERVED

McDougal Publishing is a ministry of The McDougal Foundation, Inc., a Maryland nonprofit corporation dedicated to spreading the Gospel of the Lord Jesus Christ to as many people as possible in the shortest time possible.

Published by:

McDougal Publishing
P.O. Box 3595
Hagerstown, MD 21742-3595
www.mcdougal.org

ISBN 1-58158-012-6

Printed in the United States of America
For Worldwide Distribution

Dedication

To Stephanie, my beautiful and loving wife, friend and minister, who has experienced with me the power of Christ's resurrection and the fellowship of His sufferings in the nations of the world. She has been God's gift to me since Bible school.

To our two precious girls, Tiffany Joy and Shannon Glory, who have traveled and ministered with us in many parts of the world. Shannon Glory was born with gold dust on her face as a sign of a new glory upon our lives.

To the Herzog and Esperanza families, whom we love with all our hearts.

To Ruth Heflin, whose life and friendship has been a source of great inspiration, blessing and glory. Her love for God and His people could fill volumes of books if her heart was ever written down in its entirety. I owe much to this great friend and woman of God.

To Renny and Marina McLean, for their friendship and for the glory and revelation upon their lives that they have imparted to us from the very first day we met.

To Bob Shattles and his heart for souls, and to Silvania, who paid a dear price to release this new glory. It has been a great honor to share the same platform with both of you.

To all the intercessors, friends, pastors and leaders who have experienced this new glory with us around the world.

Acknowledgments

Special thanks to our most precious intercessors Kay Hoffman and Jowan Anglin, who prayed and prophesied this book to its completion, as well as the enormous blessing they have been to our family as great intercessors and friends.

To Fred Journet, who has been a crucial help to us in freeing up our time in many practical areas of ministry so that this project could be completed.

I would also like to thank Harold McDougal for his help and wisdom in editing and quickly finishing this project (by communicating with me through e-mail as I traveled and ministered). He has done it to the glory of God.

Contents

Foreword by Ruth Ward Heflin 8

Introduction 9

Prologue 13

1. Signs and Wonders 15
2. A Harvest-Producing Rain 39
3. Creative Miracles 55
4. Spontaneous Giving 83
5. A Revival of Wisdom 111
6. Angelic Visitations 153
7. Transported in the Spirit 163
8. Miraculous Unity 189
9. A Return to Our Roots 205

Epilogue 245

Foreword by Ruth Ward Heflin

God is using David Herzog to span the continents and to span the generations in this most recent wave of glory that is sweeping the world. David's own personal hunger for God, as well as his desire to see the nations receive all that God has for them, has caused him to reach into the realms of revelation and see *Mysteries of the Glory Unveiled.*

That which he has obtained by moving into the ease of the glory, he is imparting to congregations throughout Europe and America, and those to whom he ministers are now experiencing signs, wonders and miracles as never before.

Introduction

We are feeling the first sprinkles of the greatest revival of miracles, signs and wonders ever recorded since the Book of Acts. This is the result of the glory of God being manifested upon the Earth. With this increase of signs and wonders has come new revelation and a great harvest of souls, since every great move of God naturally brings with it a new harvest.

We are seeing the restoration of the spirit of Elijah upon the Church, as was prophesied:

> *"Behold, I am going to send you Elijah the prophet before the coming of the great and terrible day of the LORD."*   Malachi 4:5, NAS

In this new move of God, there is not only an increase in signs and wonders, but there are unusual and creative miracles (including resurrections from the dead), angelic visitations, and the restoration of key revelations, mysteries and truths that have been lost through the centuries.

It has been more than fifty years now since the last great miracle revival took place and fifty years since Israel became a nation. God ordained that Jubilee, the restoration of all that has been lost, occur every fifty years. This is the time of restoration.

This wave of revival will be greater than any other because we are entering the culmination of time, when we will experience the former rains and the latter rains of revival glory combined. Some of the things we are experiencing are familiar, but many things are brand-new. This, too, was foretold in God's Word concerning the last days.

Great mysteries are being rediscovered that will unleash the greatest outpouring of God's glory and harvest since the early Church, even since the beginning of time. God's golden glory will bring in a golden harvest.

We have personally experienced several waves of revival in recent years, with miracles, signs and wonders followed by a great harvest. In one such wave, we ministered in a six-month revival meeting in Paris, France. Toward the end of that revival, the Lord told me that there was much more coming, and I began a new quest, seeking newer and greater realms of glory.

I was not disappointed. Within a few short weeks I was seeing totally new manifestations of God's glory. Those who seek the new will find it, while those who are content with their anointing and walk with God will not see the next move of God. For a move to be a move, it has to keep moving, and we must keep moving with it! The clouds of revival glory are constantly changing, and new glory cloud formations are on the horizon.

Now God is looking for those who will dare to say that there is yet another wave of greater glory in the midst of the current glory. As John the Baptist preached repentance and prepared the way for Jesus' ministry — which included miracles, signs and wonders — so the current move of holiness has greatly helped and continues to prepare the way for this exciting new move of God.

It is one thing to know about the glory, and yet another thing to have *"the knowledge of the glory."* The Bible says that *"the earth will be filled,"* not only with the glory of the Lord, but *"with the knowledge of the glory of the LORD, as the waters cover the sea"* (Habakkuk 2:14). This new flood of knowledge is unlocking hidden realms of glory, and the result is that millions of souls are pouring into the Kingdom of God.

The glory of the Lord among us is like a cloud that we see and sense, but we need to know how to get the cloud to manifest rain. It is not enough to say that the spirit of revival or glory is near or on the horizon. We need the knowledge of the glory to see the heavens opened and the *Mysteries of the Glory Unveiled*!

David Herzog
Paris, France

*"For the earth will be filled
With the knowledge of the glory of the LORD,
As the waters cover the sea."*

Habakkuk 2:14

Prologue

On a train traveling toward the city of Marseille for a preaching engagement in the south of France, I was listening to my Walkman and worshiping the Lord. I happened to look down at my hands, and they had golden flakes all over them. I ran to the rest room, only to find that the gold was also on my face.

The presence of God filled the cabin and seemed somehow fresh and new. I was in awe at the wonderful new thing that was happening in my life, and I spent the rest of the time en route to Marseille in a cloud of God's glory.

When I arrived in Marseille, the pastor of the church where I would be preaching picked me up at the train station. His first question to me was, "Have you heard about the new thing God is doing with gold dust?" For some reason, I felt restrained from immediately sharing with him my experience. I told him that I had definitely heard about it.

"Do you think it will be manifest tonight in the meeting?" he asked.

"Well, let's let God do whatever He wants to do," I answered, and the subject was dropped.

The congregation that night was made up of former rock and roll junkies and drug addicts. Many of them would receive healing and deliverance that night. I shared with them my experience with the gold dust and told them I believed it was a sign of new things coming from the Lord. Toward the end of the meeting, I noticed that the pastor's wife had gotten very excited and that people were gathering around her. Her hair was full of golden dust and flakes. Then others began seeing it come on their hands. The meeting exploded with God's glory.

1

Signs and Wonders

"The silver is Mine, and the gold is Mine," says the LORD *of hosts. "The glory of this latter temple shall be greater than the former," says the* LORD *of hosts.*
Haggai 2:8-9

When the gold dust began to appear in our ministry, we had already been seeing the Lord do some amazing things. After my wife and I had spent some years spreading renewal across America and Europe, we were powerfully touched by the Pensacola Revival, and the Lord told us that He would do a similar thing in France. We went there and began revival meetings.

The revival in Paris started, amazingly, on the same day of the year as that of the Pensacola revival, June 18. It was 1998, and for the next six months, amazing things happened.

The revival started when we conducted a forty-day prayer and fasting chain. This brought a spirit of repentance upon the Christians and caused them to come forward and publicly seek forgiveness. Many testified that their secret sins had left them with terrible guilt and shame. Now they were free.

Articles used for sin — such as pornography, drugs and drug paraphernalia, and various items used in witchcraft — were thrown on the altar each night and forsaken. God had spoken to us that believers should not only ask God to forgive their sin, but should allow Him to break the power of sin in their lives. And this He did.

When the power of sin began to break off of the church, this loosed a wave of sinners to come to the feet of Jesus and be saved. There seemed to be a magnet drawing people in night after night. Those who were saved included atheists, witches, gang members, drug addicts, nominal Christians and people of other religions. Young and old alike received Jesus as Savior. This included not only people from all over France, but people from many other parts of

Europe and the world. It was so exciting each night to see Frenchmen receiving salvation alongside Algerians, Egyptians or Africans. Every week, we baptized new converts.

There were many healings and miracles demonstrated publicly each night in these meetings. Deaf ears opened. Paralyzed people were healed. Many with incurable diseases and serious cancers were healed. Every type of miracle was seen in Paris during those days.

One night I received a word of knowledge that God was healing a woman of baldness. As it turned out, she was a woman everyone knew, an intercessor in Paris. She had wisps of thin hair, but was, for the most part, bald and sometimes used a hat or scarf to cover her baldness. She came forward in that moment, and God began to heal her right there. Within a few weeks, her hair had grown out so much that she came forward and publicly testified about the miracle.

We prayed over handkerchiefs as the early disciples had, and these were sent to the sick. A lady sent one of the prayer cloths to her father in Peru. He was dying of leukemia. The prayer cloth was placed in his bed, and the next morning he was well. There were testimonies of cancers and other sicknesses being healed in this way as well.

A Messianic Jewish man came to the meetings

from the south of France, driving about ten hours to get to Paris. He brought with him a piece of his daughter's clothing to be prayed over. She was four years old, but she could not speak or hear, and she could not eat and urinate normally. Doctors had done all they could for her, but it had not helped. We prayed over the child's clothing, and he took it back and placed it on her. Within a few days, she was totally healed. Her doctors, atheists, asked her parents to come in and explain to them just how the child had become normal.

The young people of Paris were very excited by all that was happening and went out into the streets of the city, speaking to the lost and getting them to come to the meetings. Many of those who came in in this way were won to the Lord, among them many hardened sinners.

A Declaration of Continued Revival

After four weeks of meetings, we were about to bring things to a close, when the Lord spoke to me. The World Cup soccer tournament was being played, and He told me to prophesy that France would win the World Cup as a sign of God's favor upon France and as a sign that we were to continue the revival. In a vision, He showed me Brazil handing a baton to France for revival. (Interestingly enough, the gold dust phenomenon, which started in Brazil, has now spread to every part of France, and from there to other parts of Europe.) France won the World Cup that year, and we were excited to continue the revival. We were glad we did, for in the coming weeks and months people attended from all over France, and from England, Holland, Germany, Spain and other countries.

Rising to a New Level

Toward the end of 1998, the Lord began to speak to me about another level of glory that was coming. I told Him I wanted it. He instructed me to close the revival and take several weeks off. He would use that time to place us into the new level of glory and ministry.

This was a little like sacrificing our Isaac. A long-awaited revival had come, and the last time France had experienced revival was in the 1950s. The holiness and healing ministry in that revival had birthed most of the Spirit-filled churches that existed in France. Now God had restored that which was lost, but He was telling us that He wanted to add something further to the revival.

This was a defining moment. Would we be willing to give up one level of glory and the recognition it brought to step into something yet unknown? Would we obey the Lord's voice?

I, for one, was ready. I had determined not to remain long on the same level of anointing. I was ready to take the plunge, if it meant we could move *"from glory to glory."* We closed that series of revival meetings, and I went back to the United States.

Three New Signs

The Lord told me to expect three new signs for the coming year, and that these signs would signify the next move of God for our lives. My wife and I had heard about the meetings of Ruth Ward Heflin and had read her book *Glory,* which we loved. It was reading her second book, *Revival Glory,* that prompted me to end the meetings in Paris and seek a new level of glory. Now the Lord instructed us to go to Ashland, Virginia, during the first days of January to receive the new thing He would do for us.

When I arrived at the Calvary Campground in Ashland, I was impressed by the concentration of glory in that place. I had never sensed the glory so strongly anywhere else in the world. After we met Sister Ruth that first night, she asked if I would speak the next night. I told her that I was not there to preach, but to receive. She insisted, and I was so glad she did.

When I got up to speak the next night, I practically sang my whole sermon. That was a first for me. During the service, gold dust appeared on our faces and hands. God did miracles of healing for those who came, and prophetic words were given for the camp and for our ministry.

I cannot explain the sheer joy I felt at rising to another level of glory. I felt like I was in Heaven. Since that time, I have ministered regularly at the Ashland Campground, and it has been an enormous privilege to be part of what God is doing there.

When I left the camp that first time, the Lord led me to go to Vancouver. I had no idea where exactly I was to go there. After I arrived in Vancouver, I called Information for churches, and then I asked the churches where the glory and miracles where taking place in the city. In this way, I came to a church that was just finishing a forty-week revival in which God had done many new and unusual miracles. They were experiencing instant weight loss and miraculous gold fillings and crowns.

The pastor was excited to have someone new visit the revival, especially since I had come by divine appointment. He had me minister that final night of the meeting. The glory of God in that building was so powerful that it seemed like a thick cloud enveloped us the moment we stepped inside.

Desperate for the New

When we returned to Europe, we did not feel led to concentrate on one city. God spoke to us to base ourselves near Paris, but He showed us that we were to reach out to cities across the Continent and beyond (the French-speaking world comprises a large portion of the 10/40 Window). We also wanted to be free to return to bless American cities with revival, since whatever touches America is often exported around the world.

We were looking forward to some great things in God, but for the first three months after we were back nothing new seemed to happen. We had great meetings, souls were saved, and sick people were healed, but we had experienced this before. I began to question the Lord about why things were going on much as before. His answer to me was that we were not yet desperate for the new. My attitude had been that if God wanted to do new things for us, He would do them. All the while, He was waiting for me to hunger and yearn for the new, as I had for the previous move of His Spirit.

There was another element to my hesitation. Because I did not totally understand yet the significance of the gold manifestations, I was subconsciously holding back. It was only when I heard people criticizing the new things God was doing in others, who clearly had experienced a new level of revival, that I realized where my attitude was coming from.

I was just like others. Once they had experienced a move of God, they were quick to criticize those who were experiencing something new. I vowed to fully embrace the new, regardless of what persecution or criticism might come, and I began to hunger and thirst for it as never before.

I had to go from being neutral about this manifestation to being a willing carrier of the new glory. Neutrality never wins God's heart. He said He preferred that we be either hot or cold about what we believe.

When I shifted out of neutral and put myself strongly on the Lord's side, suddenly the gold was appearing everywhere I ministered. It was on faces, hands and clothes, and it was on walls and floors.

God's Glory in Toulon

The case of Marseille was the first. The next morning, I shared in a Bible school in the neighboring town of Toulon. After a time of ministry, the Spirit of holiness pervaded the meeting, and many began to weep before the Lord. They searched their hearts, and the Holy Spirit exposed hidden motives, bitterness, rejection and other obstacles to walking in the glory of God.

After the prayer had subsided, I suddenly noticed everyone moving toward the outer walls of the building. The walls and floor were covered with gold flakes. We were all astonished.

Word quickly spread around town and into other neighboring towns, and people came from many places over the next few days to see this new sign. Some took Scotch tape and, with it, collected as many gold flakes as they could to show to others. Those whom they showed were also very excited by this new phenomenon.

These strange occurrences became our free publicity for the larger nightly meetings. As a result, many souls were saved, God gave us some wonderful miracles of healing, and the glory of God pervaded the meetings.

The interesting thing about the appearance of the gold flakes on the walls in Toulon is that those walls were covered with a red material. When the gold flakes appeared over the red, the Lord spoke clearly to us and said that the red was symbolic of the blood of Jesus, washing us and bringing a spirit of holiness, and that He was now adding a layer of signs and wonders.

My friend Debbie Kendrick once told me that when an artist wants to paint a gold frame, he first paints it red and then paints gold over the red. When it is done in this way, the gold comes out much brighter and purer.

In Strasbourg, France, gold dust appeared both inside and outside of the believers' cars for more than a month after our meetings ended there. One pastor had gold dust cover his Bible. Inside, it appeared on the page containing Haggai 2, where the Lord said, *"The silver is Mine, and the gold is Mine."*

In Amsterdam, Holland, I was invited to speak at a conference called EuroSpirit, organized by Bert Panhouise. Thousands of Dutch people were there, and they were hungry for God. Many of these later reported that they experienced the gold dust. Those meetings were televised throughout Europe.

A Revival of Signs and Wonders

A spirit of holiness has been sweeping the United States and the world in recent years, especially since the Pensacola Revival broke out. This spirit of holiness has been much like John the Baptist, preparing the way for Jesus and His miracles. John moved in holiness, preparing the way, and then Jesus came with His signs, wonders and miracles. Jesus also preached repentance, but He added this new element of the miraculous. The fact that we are seeing a whole new wave of unusual miracles has convinced me that we are entering an entirely new phase of revival.

It was at this point that John the Baptist erred. He sent messengers to ask Jesus if He really was the long-awaited Messiah. The Lord's response was quite interesting:

> *"Go and tell John the things you have seen and heard: that the blind see, the lame walk, the lepers are cleansed, the deaf hear, the dead are raised, the poor have the gospel preached to them. And blessed is he who is not offended because of Me."*   Luke 7:22-23

"Blessed is he who is not offended." It is easy to miss a new move of God or to be *"offended"* as each new move comes. It happens largely because revival takes on a different form each time it comes. Each wave is a little different. Many people, for instance, are still looking for the restoration of the 1950 Revival. While this new move of God will have many of the characteristics of that one, it will also have many new elements.

God seems to package revival in such a way as to attract only those who are desperate for Him. The hungry are somehow able to see what God is doing through strange new circumstances, rather than judging by outward appearances. When people are expecting God to bring revival in the way they have known in the past (and it comes in a totally different form), it seems easy for them to reject it. The sad thing is that they just keep waiting for something else to come along.

We must be careful. That which we reject may very well be the beginning of what we have been waiting and praying for. The people of Israel were waiting for their Messiah, but when He showed up in a most unexpected way, the religious community rejected Him. Despite the great things Jesus did, the Jewish people of His day somehow could not recognize that He was what they had prayed and hoped for for so long.

When Jesus came, He did many unusual signs, not just those that are recorded in the Bible:

> *Therefore many other signs Jesus also performed in the presence of the disciples, which are not written in this book.*
>
> John 20:30, NNAS

I am convinced that in the days ahead we will see many of the same miracles that accompanied Jesus while He was on the Earth, and the signs and wonders we see will also be too many and too diverse to be recorded.

We were experiencing the first sign, the gold dust, regularly now, but where was the second sign?

The Second Sign

At the conference in Amsterdam, I met a Dutchman whom God had been using to give His people golden fillings in their teeth. I asked him to pray for me. The next day I spoke in a church in the city before going to the airport to fly back to Paris. I had only thirty minutes to preach, but in those few minutes God did amazing things for the people.

First, gold dust began to appear all over their faces. Then a man screamed out, "I have a gold tooth!" His tooth had been crowned with gold. From then on, we have been seeing more and more of this supernatural manifestation.

Later, when I was preaching at the Summer Campmeeting in Ashland, several times we saw more than a hundred teeth turned to gold in a few minutes. The people ran to the front to testify.

Souls were saved in all of these meetings, and many were healed. Every time we have seen this manifestation, the atmosphere has proven to be charged for miracles.

In Flagstaff, Arizona, gold dust appeared and many gold and silver fillings were received. One lady, whose shoes were silver, had them covered with gold. The gold and silver were interwoven into a pattern. The same lady had a silver watch, and the back of her watch was covered with gold so that no silver was visible.

Again many souls were saved as a result of these miracles, including a homosexual and a couple involved in the New Age movement and drugs. Native American Indians came into that meeting and were saved as well.

The man in the couple was an American, and his wife was from Montreal, Canada. I had received, only a few days before, an invitation to preach in Montreal, and I accepted the salvation of this woman as a sign that I should accept that invitation. Her salvation was the firstfruits of what awaited me there.

When I went to Montreal, her entire family came to the meetings, and several of them received salvation after seeing the signs and wonders God was doing.

A First in Montreal, in Ireland, in Scotland, and in Israel

When gold dust fell in the meetings in Montreal, it was the first time this phenomenon had been reported in French Canada. Many spontaneous miracles took place in those meetings without my having to lay hands on the people.

One of the exceptional cases was a paralyzed boy who walked for the first time in his life. Everyone present witnessed this miracle, and they were all weeping and shouting with joy.

The evangelist of that church, Luigi, helped me to walk the boy around just before he was healed. Afterward, Luigi himself came to me for prayer, and I prophesied over him that he would raise the dead. The next week he prayed over a dead woman, and she came back to life. This happened in the presence of five doctors who had tried in vain to revive the woman.

Gold dust also appeared when we ministered in a church in Ottawa pastored by Jean Turpin.

In a church in Heidelberg, Germany, pastored by Pierrot Fey, oil began to pour from people's hands while I was ministering. Later, two teenage girls, who were visitors to the church, saw people receiving gold fillings. They went right home to share this with their parents, who were also pastors. As the girls began to tell about what they had seen, gold dust began to come upon the parents too.

In Ireland, gold dust fell for the first time and gold teeth were received during a singles' retreat. We witnessed a lady's jewelry turn from silver to gold right in front of our eyes. Many physical healings and miracles took place, and the people were possessed of a spirit of spontaneous giving. Souls were saved, and many experienced deliverance from bondages.

After the retreat, the people who had attended the conference spread the news of these signs and wonders throughout the countryside. Many of them used it as an evangelistic tool. Some even told their bosses. One lady went into a store, and the owner of the store noticed the gold on her and asked her about it. She was able to effectively preach the Gospel in that store, and signs and wonders followed her there.

A lady who had received many gold fillings and crowns in the meetings went about showing them to everyone and testifying to them. She invited her unsaved friends to look into her mouth and see if they saw anything different. When they noticed the new teeth, she used that to lead her friends to the Lord. Signs and wonders are great tools for winning the lost.

In Scotland, we again saw the gold manifestations come for the first time that we know of in that country. It happened in Aberdeen. One lady was missing an entire tooth and had a large gap between her teeth. God miraculously put a tooth where there had been none. We were all amazed.

Several ladies there experienced instant weight loss, going down several dress sizes. They came forward to demonstrate their now baggy clothes. One even brought a scale up to the front to show everyone that she had indeed lost weight miraculously. As you can imagine, souls were gloriously saved in those meetings.

In Tel Aviv, Israel, God did the same miracles.

Many people received gold fillings and crowns, including the pastors. Russian Jews reported that several of them saw the living Messiah walk into the meeting. They were stunned. One night, during a time of intercession, gold dust fell upon the congregation. It was the first time this phenomenon had been reported in Tel Aviv.

In Jerusalem, at Mount Zion Fellowship, gold teeth were manifested, and in Christ Church near the Jaffa Gate, a Jewish woman received a gold tooth for the first time in that church.

Sephardic Jews See Signs and Wonders

After the meeting in Tel Aviv, we went to visit one of the leaders of the congregation who was in the hospital recuperating from surgery. We all showed him our new teeth. The man in the next bed and those who were visiting him were wondering what could be so exciting about teeth. I began to share with them what God was doing.

Most of them were Sephardic Jews, and one of them, a chemical engineer, said what I was saying was impossible. "Men have been trying to change one metal into another for years," he told me, "and they have not been able to do it."

"I agree that it is impossible," I assured him, "but the things that are impossible with men are possible with God." I reminded him that millions of Jewish people had lost their teeth under the Nazis during World War II. "Now," I said, "God is restoring what was lost."

He could relate to what I was saying. Swiss banks are finally recognizing the heirs of confiscated bank accounts, and properties and works of art are being returned to the families who originally owned them. Fifty years have gone by since the war, but this is the time of Jubilee, the time of restoration. The man was touched and agreed to invite the Jewish Messiah, Yeshua, into his heart that evening.

Paul wrote:

Jews demand miraculous signs.
1 Corinthians 1:22, NIV

The revival of signs and wonders is the most powerful and biblical way to witness to Jews and Muslims. After all, this is the way Jesus did it.

Holland, Phoenix and French Guiana

This ministry has not abated, but only increased. Recently I ministered in Holland again. Not only did the gold dust come on people's hands, faces, Bibles and clothes, but even a diamond appeared. A jeweler who was in attendance came forward and examined it with his loupe. He was impressed and said it was a perfectly good diamond.

A lady from Iran gave her life to the Lord in that meeting as a result of these signs and wonders. More than four hundred young people from all over Holland attended, and many of them came to know the Lord. They stayed until four o'clock in the morning weeping for souls. By the time they had finished their intercession, gold had covered the floor where they were praying. In the days following these meetings, many of these young people found their unsaved friends and family members strangely open to the Gospel.

In Phoenix, Arizona, I shared on the local Christian television station (TBN) about these new miracles and prayed for the people. Several days later, some who were watching a rerun of the telecast reported receiving gold and silver fillings in the shape of a cross.

In French Guiana, gold dust and gold fillings and crowns were received in the meetings we conducted in Cayenne and Korou. It was again the first time it had happened there. The pastor had four teeth filled and crowned.

My wife has two gold fillings from those meetings. Many other people had their teeth changed as a sign and a wonder. After the floor of the church was cleaned, the vacuum cleaner was found to be full of gold dust.

In the jungle area of French Guiana, near the Amazon, God did amazing things. Not only did gold dust appear, but also dust and flakes of green, blue and red, and what looked like diamond, crystal and copper. Our arms were covered with flakes of many colors, as was the floor. Many came forward to receive Jesus, some of whom had been involved in serious witchcraft.

The Importance of the River

I couldn't help but notice how important the river running through that area was to the life of the people. It was their principal route for transportation and their principal source for food. They even found it indispensable for bathing. It reminded me of another river God's Word describes:

> *Now a river went out of Eden to water the garden, and from there it parted and became four riverheads. The name of the first is Pishon; it is the one which skirts the whole land of Havilah, where there is gold. And the gold of that land is good. Bdellium and the onyx stone are there.*
> Genesis 2:10

A new river was running through French Guiana, the river of God's glory, and the gold of it was likewise "good."

And that is just the beginning of the story. If all the details were told, as in the case of the *"many other things which Jesus did,"* the details would fill many volumes:

> And there are also many other things which
> Jesus did, which if they were written in detail,
> I suppose that even the world itself would not
> contain the books that would be written.
>
> John 21:25, NNAS

Why the Gold?

Many are asking what all this means, and it is a legitimate question. Our second child, Shannon Glory, was born at the beginning of all of this manifestation, and Debbie Kendrick prophesied that she would be "a sign and a wonder." When Shannon was born, there was gold dust all over her face, and she continues to have this manifestation to this day.

How can this be explained? Isaiah foretold:

> And His glory will be seen upon you.
>
> Isaiah 60:2

Moses had a visible manifestation of the glory when his face shone. Many others in the Bible experienced the same thing. The Bible foretold that great signs and wonders would be seen in the last days, and this is one of them. Since God is still a Creator, He is still in the business of creating new things. Each new move of His Spirit has its own mark upon it.

The gold dust is not an end in itself. It is only a sign of what is to come. When the gold appears, it is an indication that the atmosphere in a meeting is charged for miracles, and anything can happen. This is the same anointing in which Elijah and Jesus operated. They performed miracles, signs and wonders, raised the dead, and saw miraculous provision. By sending this unusual manifestation into our midst, God is saying to us that we can expect to see the same things.

2

A Harvest-Producing Rain

Ask the LORD *for rain*
In the time of the latter rain.
The LORD *will make flashing*
clouds;
He will give them showers of
rain,
Grass in the field for everyone.
                    Zechariah 10:1

Most of use who are attuned to God's Spirit have come to believe that a great harvest of souls is on His immediate agenda, and we have become very interested in the subject of harvest. Throughout history, great outpourings of the Holy Spirit have been accompanied by a great harvest of souls.

The first such outpouring took place, of course, on the Day of Pentecost, and it is recorded in the Book of Acts. That day, people were refreshed, revived, empowered and filled with joy. Soon thereafter, three thousand souls were saved, and this great harvest of souls continued in the fledgling Church on a daily basis.

As the harvest grew ever larger, some in the affected areas became alarmed, and persecution broke out against the Church. This resulted in the disciples needing another wave of empowerment, so that they could remain faithful to God. In response, He sent them another refreshing rain:

> *And when they had prayed, the place where they were assembled together was shaken; and they were all filled with the Holy Spirit, and they spoke the word of God with boldness.*

> Acts 4:31

Each time the Holy Spirit is poured out over a thirsty land, it produces a harvest. In the Book of Acts, we can see the progression of the revival:

> *And the Lord ADDED TO THE CHURCH DAILY those who were being saved.*

> Acts 2:47

And believers were THE MORE ADDED TO THE LORD, multitudes both of men and women. Acts 5:14, KJV

Then the churches throughout all Judea, Galilee, and Samaria had peace and were edified. And walking in the fear of the Lord and in the comfort of the Holy Spirit, THEY WERE MULTIPLIED. Acts 9:31

Each wave of outpouring brought with it a wave of harvest, each increase in the power of God bringing an increase in the number of souls saved.

The Azusa Street Revival of the early years of the twentieth century was an outpouring of the Holy Spirit that brought with it a new surge of power and the baptism of the Holy Spirit. This led to great harvest around the world.

Statistics reveal that by 1990, more than 372 million people had been affected by this outpouring. It was the foundation upon which the Pentecostal and Charismatic movements would stand.

In more recent revivals, or "renewals" or "refreshings," as many call them, again many have been saved. The revival in Pensacola is a good example of this. Evangelist Steve Hill had seen a great move of God in Argentina, but he was thirsty for more. He attended a renewal meeting in England and received a new outpouring of the Holy Spirit. This led to the Pensacola Revival, which began shortly afterward, and hundreds of thousands have been saved as a result.

A New Harvest Requires a New Rain

Now we are engaged in another great outpouring, and it too is bringing with it a great and mighty harvest. This will surely be the harvest of all harvests, and because of that, a special type of rain is now falling upon us. In meetings around the world, golden rain is falling upon those who are hungry and thirsty for God.

We had grown accustomed to speaking in tongues, to receiving joy from the new wine, to shaking and falling under the power of the Spirit, but now another manifestation has come. Who could have anticipated that God would do this? As always, He is full of surprises. He is raining His glory down over His people.

Recently, I was in meetings with Pastor Bob Shattles in Ashland, Virginia. Always a soul-winner, Pastor Shattles, a Southern Baptist, made his own trek to the Pensacola Revival, and there received a new touch of glory upon his life. With the help of Carey Robertson from Pensacola, Pastor

Shattles' Baptist church near Atlanta, Georgia, conducted a lengthy revival meeting in which it experienced phenomenal growth.

Pastor Shattles, however, was not satisfied. When he heard about this new manifestation of God's glory, he wanted it. He invited Ruth Ward Heflin to speak in his church, and when she did, gold dust began to manifest itself in his ministry. It happened not only when he was in his church but everywhere else he went.

A little more than a year later, Bob Shattles has already won fifty thousand souls to Christ as a result of this manifestation. When I was with him in those meetings in Ashland, I witnessed a golden rain falling in a column just in front of us on the platform. No wonder souls are moved to come to Christ!

Several thousand of the souls won by Bob Shattles have come to the Lord, not in churches, but in airports, restaurants, hotels and other public places. People going about their everyday tasks have been won to Christ as a result of seeing the golden glory manifested on his person.

We have experienced this golden rain in our meetings in such places as France (when my wife was ministering in a women's meeting) and Holland, and each time it has happened, it was accompanied by a great harvest. This harvest continued long after we were gone. The outpouring of the Spirit prepares the fertile ground, and like Bob Shattles, we have seen more souls saved in recent times than ever before.

Whether we actually see the golden rain falling in our services or not, it is an indication to all of us that a spiritual rain has come to bring a new harvest. Moses foretold this rain of the Spirit:

> *"Then he will continue to send both the early and late rains that will produce wonderful crops of grain."*   Deuteronomy 11:14, TLB

The Grain Has Ripened

Gold is the color of harvest. Wheat, especially, when it is ready to collect, has a beautiful golden color. As God pours out His Spirit in this unusual way, the golden glory is attracting people in record numbers. This has proven to be a most powerful tool for evangelism. People are curious, and this manifestation draws the curious.

But there are other reasons. The gold is a visible sign that the glory of God has returned to His people, and that glory draws men and women. Men who have *"sinned and come short of the glory of God"* are drawn to it when they hear that it has appeared. When they see it manifested, they are drawn to repentance and are saved. The prophet foretold:

Arise, shine;
For your light has come!
And the glory of the Lord *is risen upon you.*
Isaiah 60:1

When the glory of God is seen upon us, people are attracted to it like metal to a magnet. This makes it easy for us to bring in the harvest. It is just as God showed Isaiah it would be:

The Gentiles shall come to your light,
And kings to the brightness of your rising.
"Lift up your eyes all around, and see;
They all gather together, they come to you;
Your sons shall come from afar,
And your daughters shall be nursed at your side."
Isaiah 60:3-4

The manifestation of the glory of God leads to a harvest of souls, the rain of the Spirit producing a bumper crop.

Last summer, when I ministered in Chicago, many teeth were filled and crowned with gold, gold dust fell in the meetings, and there were many creative miracles. As we worshiped, I saw the glory of God extend outside the church into the streets, and I prophesied that drug addicts would be drawn to the glory and be saved.

Within about fifteen minutes, an addict walked into the church and made his way to the front to testify. I thought he was a member of the church who had gotten healed, so I asked him what God had done for him. He said that something had drawn him into the church as he was walking past. The moment he walked into the building, the Holy Spirit seized him, and he gave his life to the Lord.

Later, this man testified that he believed he had been instantly delivered from drugs at the moment the Holy Spirit had taken hold of his life. For good measure, we led him in a public prayer of salvation.

A few minutes later, another man came up to the front. He, too, was a drug addict and had just walked in off the street. He said he had seen the lights of the church from outside and thought it was a night club, especially when he saw some of the people dancing before the Lord. He, too, was convicted of sin the moment he walked in, and he had come to the front to be saved. Many others were saved during the altar calls.

Each week we are seeing an increase in the number of souls saved, and it is happening with such ease. It is beyond our expectations. I have never seen a greater evangelistic tool. We often sing, "We need the latter rain." We need it to facilitate the harvest.

Recently, I was preaching in Haag, Holland. One night while I was there, I had a dream of golden rain coming down so thick it seemed like snow. The next morning I shared my dream in the meetings. As I did, gold flakes began to appear everywhere. One lady had her Bible covered with gold. People saw it all over the carpet, on the chairs, on the floor, and on their hands and faces. It was then that a girl found the diamond I mentioned. It was not a small one, and, as I said, the jeweler who looked at it with his instrument told us it was real. These manifestations resulted in many finding Christ as their Savior. Among them was a precious woman from Iran.

The Elijahs in Our Midst

I believe that we have only scratched the surface. God wants to manifest His glory more and more with signs and wonders for the sake of the harvest.

Some only see the dryness of the hour, but those who have a heart toward the Spirit can see a cloud of refreshing approaching, as did the prophet Elijah:

> [Elijah] said to his servant, "Go up now, look toward the sea."
> So he went up and looked, and said, "There is nothing." And seven times he said, "Go again."
> 1 Kings 18:43

The land was in a long period of drought, which

had produced widespread famine, but Elijah began
to declare that a new outpouring of rain would soon
come. In the Spirit, he could hear something, *"the
sound of abundance of rain"* (1 Kings 18:41).

Refusing to look at circumstances, Elijah went to
the top of Mount Carmel and began to pray. As he
bowed on the ground, with his face between his
knees, God began to show him something, and the
air suddenly filled with expectancy. I understand
what Elijah was feeling that day. I feel something in
the air around us. We are about to reap the greatest
harvest of souls the world has ever seen, and it will
happen because we experience the greatest outpouring of the Spirit ever seen.

Some, as we have seen, are still looking for the
return of a former revival. Some are like the servant
who went out and looked seven times and saw nothing promising. But how can we deny that we have
already experienced the first drops of rain? We have
already reaped the firstfruits of our prayers. Miracle
revival is coming, for the sign of it, the first drops of
golden rain, has appeared.

If you have looked seven times and haven't seen
anything promising, look again:

> Then it came to pass the seventh time, that he
> said, "There is a cloud, as small as a man's
> hand, rising out of the sea!" So he said, "Go

> *up, say to Ahab, 'Prepare your chariot, and go
> down before the rain stops you.' "*
>
> 1 Kings 18:44

A cloud *"as small as a man's hand"* probably did not impress the servant, but it excited Elijah because he knew what it represented. Many have been diligently praying for great miracles and great harvest, and now, finally, we have the firstfruits of our long-sought miracle revival. The golden rain we are experiencing is often in very tiny droplets. It is not even as large as a man's hand, but we know what it represents. Good things are on the way. Who can deny it?

Differing Reactions to Today's Signs

People react to God's signs in different ways. Elijah got excited and began to proclaim that rain was on the way. He instructed his servant to get into his chariot and ride to take the news to Ahab. He was sure that the miracle was at hand.

Many people, no doubt, would not have acted on such minimal assurance. They would have waited for something more substantial to come along. People who are slow to respond to the rain of God's Spirit may miss this outpouring and have to wait for another. I feel sorry for these people because they will have to survive on the leftovers from a previous harvest, rather than rejoice in the bounty of a new one.

Respond to the signs God is sending and rejoice in them, no matter how insignificant you might consider them to be. Many people could not accept Jesus just because He was born in a stable. They let Him pass their way without their being affected by His power. When God has sent a new wave of His glory, it has often been through something seemingly foolish. He uses the simple to confound the wise and haughty. Receive it nevertheless.

The presence of clouds does not always guarantee rain. It depends on the amount of atmospheric pressure on the clouds. Our desperate hunger and thirst for God will cause His rain to come. We must respond to Him with great longing and faith, believing that what will soon follow is a great cloudburst of rain and a resulting harvest.

Whether you choose to believe it or not, we are on the verge of the greatest harvest of souls that mankind has ever witnessed. It will happen because God is confirming His Word with miracles, signs and wonders. These will even surpass those witnessed by the believers of the first century. They will be greater than anything ever witnessed anywhere on Earth.

The Elijah Anointing

God has promised that the Church would return to the spirit of Elijah, and we must be able to discern the signs of the times, as Elijah did. It is no surprise that God is using prophetic ministries, like that of Ruth Ward Heflin and others like her, to host such a move of His Spirit:

> *"Behold, I will send you Elijah the prophet*
> *Before the coming of the great and dreadful day*
> *   of the* LORD.*"*   Malachi 4:5

When Jesus was walking the Earth, men tried to label the type of revival He was bringing:

> *When Jesus came into the region of Caesarea*
> *Philippi, He asked His disciples, saying, "Who*
> *do men say that I, the Son of Man, am?"*
> *So they said, "Some say John the Baptist, some*
> *Elijah, and others Jeremiah or one of the proph-*
> *ets."*   Matthew 16:13-14

Why would Jesus have been mistaken as John, Elijah or Jeremiah? Perhaps because He took on the mantles of those men, who all spearheaded revival and soul harvests. These are mantles that we must also assume.

We have been taught for many years the importance of weeping for souls, getting a burden for nations and cities, and this typified the ministry of Jeremiah. Jesus had great compassion for souls and wept for the city of Jerusalem.

We have had a resurgence of the spirit of holiness and repentance, most recently during the Pensacola Revival (which is still continuing), and this typified the mantle of John the Baptist. Jesus preached repentance, just as John did. Some even thought that He was John risen from the dead.

Elijah confronted and challenged the sorcerers of his day with greater miracles, signs and wonders, causing great revival. He raised the dead, healed the sick, had authority over nature, and performed many unusual miracles — beginning and ending with provisional miracles.

Jesus came in that same anointing. He raised Lazarus from the dead, multiplied bread and turned water into wine, healed the sick, and challenged every power and authority of His day.

The apostles continued in Jesus' footsteps, and the same glory that empowered them is at work again today. The Elijah anointing is now coming upon the Church.

Boldness Required

Will we press into this next move of God? Or will

we shrink back and let someone else pioneer the last-day harvest? God is looking for those who will be bold enough to go from one level of blessing to another and take the risks necessary to experience yet another great move of His Spirit. Joel declared:

> *Be glad then, you children of Zion,*
> *And rejoice in the LORD your God;*
> *For He has given you the former rain faithfully,*
> *And He will cause the rain to come down for*
> *you —*
> *The former rain,*
> *And the latter rain in the first month.*
> Joel 2:23

God has always been faithful to send us the rain for the harvest. We must receive it with joy so that the next harvest will come. We will see the restoration of the former rain and the latter rain combined. As we have seen, some characteristics of this current move of God will resemble past revivals, but many things will be totally new. One thing is certain, a great harvest will be reaped as a result. As Joel declared:

> *The threshing floors shall be full of wheat,*
> *And the vats shall overflow with new wine and*
> *oil.*   Joel 2:24

Our desperate hunger and thirst for God's manifest presence will put the atmospheric pressure upon the clouds that are over us even now, and the rains will surely come:

> *"And it shall come to pass afterward*
> *That I will pour out My Spirit on all flesh; ...*
> *And I will show wonders in the heavens and in*
> *the earth."*   Joel 2:28-30

Get ready. The rain is coming.

3

Creative Miracles

In the beginning God created.
Genesis 1:1

God has not changed. As He created *"in the beginning,"* He continues to create today. Unusual creative miracles are increasingly manifest in meetings where the gold dust is falling. This is nothing new, and should not be considered unnatural. To the contrary, this is the natural result of the rain of God's glory coming upon the Church.

A miracle is understood by most people to mean some sort of divine intervention. Our God has been intervening in the affairs of man since the beginning of time, so miracles should be an everyday occurrence for those of us who believe.

The best place to look in the Bible for understanding concerning the realm of creative miracles is the Book of Genesis, the book of beginnings. This book is a record of the first creative miracles done by the hand of God Almighty. It begins with His creation of the world as we know of it:

> *In the beginning God created the heavens and the earth. The earth was empty, a formless mass cloaked in darkness. And the Spirit of God was hovering over its surface. Then God said, "Let there be light," and there was light.*
>
> Genesis 1:1-3, NLT

The Key to Creative Miracles

"The Spirit of God was hovering over its surface." This is the most important secret we can learn about operating in creative miracles. When the presence of God, His glory, begins to hover over a place or a person, the power and potential for creative miracles is present. Releasing this working of cre-

ative miracles must be done while the Spirit is hovering in this way. It is an act so simple that most of us miss it.

While the Spirit hovered, God the Father spoke. He said, *"Let there be light,"* and when He said that, light was created. Everything that God created was created in this same way. God spoke it into being. Every living thing was spoken into being by God.

As the crowning glory of His creation, God made us. We are created in His image and were meant to be His representatives on the Earth. We can now speak on His behalf. We can declare what He shows us He wants to do.

When the presence of God is hovering over you in a given place, and you hear His voice saying something like "cancers are dissolving" or "limbs are growing back," you must do what God did. You must speak those words out. Learn to do it spontaneously as He is saying it, and when you do, creative miracles will begin to manifest themselves.

If we stop to analyze what we are hearing in such moments (out of fear), and we hesitate or procrastinate, the moment can be lost. The quicker we act on what God is saying, the more easily and dramatically the creative miracle will occur. This is especially true when God is saying something that seems absolutely impossible or beyond our faith level.

Going Beyond the Limitation of Our Own Faith

This is an important point. The things God is calling us to do in the realm of creative miracles are always beyond our faith level. So, even though we sense that the glory of God is hovering over us, it is easy to let our reasoning get in the way of action. In these moments, it is no longer a question of having enough faith to do the miracle. The only question is: Who is speaking? We might also ask: Will we rise to the challenge?

When we become convinced that the Creator Himself is speaking through us, we know that all we must do is obey. We use our faith to tap into God's glory, but once we do, acting creatively demands that we only listen and obey. The work to be done is a work of the Creator. It is His glory that does the work, not anything that we can do ourselves.

When we learn to speak before we have had the chance to analyze the impossibility of what we are saying, the miracle is already done. Jesus expressed it in this way:

> "My sheep hear My voice, and I know them, and they follow Me."   John 10:27

Entering the creative realm, then, is as simple as hearing the Lord and following His instructions.

The power of God's spoken word is awesome. It is eternal. It is creative. After God spoke the planets and the galaxies into existence, His word did not suddenly become powerless. He is still capable of creation, and when we believe Him, He still creates.

Scientists tell us that there are "new" planets and galaxies. These did not previously exist, but they are even now being created. The universe is still expanding, and it is doing so at the speed of light.

Light was the first thing God created on the Earth, and light is symbolic of His glory. Again, Isaiah declared:

> *Arise, shine; for your light has come!*
> *And the glory of the* LORD *is risen upon you.*
>   Isaiah 60:1

Scientists have come to use the speed at which light travels (the speed of light) as a scientific measurement. But light is only symbolic of God's glory, and the speed of light is but a shadow of the speed of God's glory. Miracles are created at the speed of glory, for in the glory there is no limit of time as we know it.

Soaring Effortlessly

Consider the space shuttle being sent into Earth orbit. It requires huge amounts of power to launch it out into space. Once it is able to escape the gravity of the Earth, however, the shuttle moves about effortlessly in space.

Let's say that the space shuttle is your faith. It may take an effort for you to get yourself launched into the realm of the miraculous, but once you are there, you no longer require the same effort. The pull of gravity is gone, and you now find yourself in a very different atmosphere, one that does not require of you the same effort that was necessary to get you there in the first place.

Most of us can get our faith only as high as the sky. We are able to fly like an airplane, but as long as we are in control, we are limited. It is only when we can leave the confines of our own limited faith and tap into the resources of God's limitless faith that we can begin to operate in creative miracles.

An airplane will eventually run out of fuel, but a spaceship can drift in orbit effortlessly for much longer periods. This is why it is possible to feel tired (some say "burned-out") after a very anointed time of ministry. When the glory of God is present, fatigue is never a factor, and hours seems like minutes. In the glory, we are no longer working. God is doing the work, so we don't get tired, as we would without the glory.

Why Miracles Sometimes Don't Happen

Sometimes we use our faith to speak things we

would like to see happen, or we lay hands on people
we would like to see healed or delivered. If we were
to be honest, we would have to say that our ministry results sometimes seem to be hit-and-miss. We
do not receive total victory for every person we pray
for. This leads us to wonder how Jesus achieved instant and total results when He ministered to the
people of His day:

> *Great multitudes followed Him, and HE*
> *HEALED THEM ALL.*   Matthew 12:15

What was the secret of the Lord's one hundred
percent instant results? He said:

> *As the Father gave me commandment, even so*
> *I do.*   John 14:31, KJV

Tapping into the glory requires doing what the
Father commands. It is His command that is powerful, not ours. It is His command that is creative,
not ours:

> *He issued his command, and they came into*
> *being.*   Psalm 148:5, NLT

When God speaks and we simply say or do what
He is saying or doing, spontaneous miracles occur.

God spoke and He created in Genesis, and the pattern of creation has not changed.

Someone might argue that God has already given us the privilege of laying hands on the sick and seeing miracles of healing performed. Why do we need something more? I believe it is a question of "good," "better," and "best." We can act on our faith, lay hands on the sick, and expect them to recover. These are good methods of ministry, and we will not abandon them. But neither should we be limited by them. If we use our faith as a tool to tap into the glory, not as an end in itself, we can rise to higher levels of God's presence and power.

Our Work vs God's Work

God's anointing was given to us so that we could do His *"works"* (John 9:4), and when we work, we get tired.

Before the fall, Adam and Eve were not required to earn their living by the sweat of their brows. Plants grew and produced fruit, with no toil or sweat required on man's part. Adam and Eve only had to manage the garden. It was the fall that changed all that.

In this same way, the anointing and even faith were given to man after the fall to get him back into the glory of God. The anointing is to do the *"works"* of the ministry, and there will be no need for faith *or* the anointing in Heaven. Heaven is filled with God's glory, and there all toil will cease. It takes faith and the anointing to get into the glory, but once we are there, toil is no longer required.

The glory of God was in the Garden of Eden before the fall. God only had to speak, and things were created. When we tap into this same glory, we no longer have to do the work. God does it.

The choice is ours. We can work hard and stay in faith and see good results, or we can use our faith to rise into the glory realm. Once there, as we do and say what we see God doing and saying, there will be immediate and lasting results.

The Faith Realm vs the Glory Realm

Heaven is filled with God's glory. There will be no sickness there. Therefore when we speak a word of healing or miracles in the glory, there are instant results. Wonderful things can be done in the faith realm, but greater things can be done in the glory realm.

I have seen cancers fall off, deaf ears pop open, bald heads grow hair, and a multitude of other miracles happen simply by speaking what I heard at that moment. I have seen teeth filled and crowned with gold over and over again, as I heard God say it, and I began to declare it.

True, I have also seen similar results with the laying on of hands, but I have noticed that many more people are healed by the spoken word of God than through the laying on of hands. And it happens much more quickly.

When we are in meetings with thousands of people, it is even physically difficult to lay hands on everyone. We can speak a word that we hear from Heaven, and instantly hundreds can be healed at one time.

Laying hands on everyone is an acceptable method for bringing healing, but it is very tiring to lay hands on everyone when there is a large group. We must not allow our limitations to prevent us from having God's best. Tap into all His resources and experience His miracles.

The writer of the Letter to the Hebrews hinted at this progression:

> *Therefore, leaving the discussion of the elementary principles of Christ, let us go on to perfection, not laying again the foundation of repentance from dead works and OF FAITH TOWARD GOD, of the doctrine of baptisms, OF LAYING ON OF HANDS, of resurrection of the dead, and of eternal judgment.*
>
> Hebrews 6:1-2

Responding to the Spoken Word

Our spontaneous obedience to what God is telling us to do or say determines whether or not miracles will actually be manifested:

> *"Time and again I warned you about what was going to happen in the future. Then suddenly I took action, and all my predictions came true."*
> Isaiah 48:3, NLT

When a prophetic word is spoken, for example, concerning healings and miracles, someone's calling and destiny, or a financial miracle, that thing has been created the moment it was spoken. We often wait for it to become apparent, not realizing that the moment it was spoken it already came into being. This is true — whether we see the thing or not. It is like a picture frame that has been created for us by God. It's there, and He is waiting for us to step into the frame and complete the picture.

Whatever God says to you, do it. When you delay and wait for the manifestation of what has been spoken, the matter is suspended and can stay that way if there is no response on your part. Through Isaiah, the Lord said, *"Suddenly I took action, and [then] all my predictions came true."* Take action, and your predictions will come true too.

This word *suddenly* means "spontaneously" or "instantaneously." That is how quickly we need to follow God's commands. The longer we delay, the more we will reason things out, and this will probably lead to our not acting at all. Start walking into the frame of what God has told you, and you will see that it has been there all along.

When the virgin Mary heard the prophetic word that she would carry the Messiah in her womb, she immediately responded:

> "I am the Lord's servant, and I am willing to accept whatever he wants. May everything you have said come true."   Luke 1:38, NLT

Mary's response was immediate and positive, and I believe that the moment she responded in this way, walking into the frame God had made for her, the child Jesus began to be formed in her womb. The proof is that the very next verse affirms that she was pregnant *"a few days later"*:

> A few days later Mary hurried to the hill country of Judea, to the town where Zechariah lived. ... At the sound of Mary's greeting, Elizabeth's child leaped within her, and Elizabeth was filled with the Holy Spirit.
> Elizabeth gave a glad cry and exclaimed to

Mary, "You are blessed by God above all other women, and your child is blessed."
Luke 1:39-42, NLT

Another amazing thing happened that day, when John the Baptist leaped in his mother's womb. His little spirit (certainly not his human reasoning) responded to the glory in the Baby Jesus. In that moment, the prophecies over John became sealed.

The Power of the Tongue

Zechariah, John's father, had not responded nearly as well when God spoke to him through an angel in the Temple. He questioned what was said and tried to reason it out, rather than spontaneously accepting and responding to it. The result was that God allowed him to become mute.

If the priest would not use His tongue to create, to bring life and to walk into the frame God had created for him, God would take away his ability to speak. Zechariah was in danger of hindering the prophetic word, and God took these drastic measures to prevent the man from thwarting His plan. He would remain in silence as Elizabeth conceived and the child grew and would speak again only after John was born.

The Bible declares that the power of life and death is resident in the tongue:

Death and life are in the power of the tongue.
                              Proverbs 18:21

Isaiah recorded the Lord's words:

*"You have heard my predictions and seen them
fulfilled, but you refuse to admit it."*
                              Isaiah 48:6, NLT

God was asking, "Will you not declare what I predict?" Start declaring and responding to what you see and hear from Heaven. When we only do and say what we hear our Father saying (as Jesus did), trusting not in our own reasoning or logic, but trusting in Him, His promises come into being quickly and easily.

Future or Present Tense?

Usually we think of prophetic words as being in the future tense. We need to change that mind-set. Whether a word is in future tense or present tense depends on us. Once it is spoken, it is there to be walked into. The Lord spoke through Isaiah of doing things *"RIGHT NOW"*:

*"For I am ready to set things right, NOT IN
THE DISTANT FUTURE, BUT RIGHT
NOW!"*   Isaiah 46:13, NLT

What has God promised to you? Whatever it is, it already exists. It was created when He spoke it.

It is no longer a question of when the promise of God will come to pass. The question now is: When will you start walking into it? Once you have the understanding that it already exists, you have faith to walk into it.

The Word of God tells us that Jesus is *"the Lamb slain from the foundation of the world"* (Revelation 13:8). On the cross of Calvary, He walked into what had already been prepared for Him.

Paul spoke of this act of walking into our promised destiny:

> *For we are His workmanship, created in Christ Jesus for good works, which God prepared beforehand that we should walk in them.*
>
> Ephesians 2:10

Begin to walk into that which God has already spoken and prepared for you. It's waiting.

In the summer of 1999, when I was ministering at the campground in Ashland, Virginia, the Lord told me to prophesy over Ruth Heflin. What came out of my mouth surprised me, yet I obeyed without trying to understand it first. I declared that soon she would speak with the Pope and that this encounter would cause an open door in the Spirit, resulting in the salvation of millions of Catholics.

No sooner had I spoken this word than Ruth confirmed that she had recently had a divine connection with someone who said he would work on setting up a visit for her with the Pope. Just recently, I got word that when the Pope visited Israel, Ruth was one of his invited guests, thus fulfilling the prophecy.

It is amazing how fast God brings major events together in His glory. I believe that as we are faithful to speak and declare that which may sound unusual or unbelievable, God begins to bring the situation into being — without our minds having to understand how He does it.

Miracles Manifest the Glory

Miracles are a manifestation of the glory of God. When Jesus raised Lazarus by the spoken word, He did it to manifest the glory that was already present:

> *When Jesus heard that, He said, "This sickness is not unto death, but for the glory of God, that the Son of God may be glorified through it."*
> John 11:4

Later, Jesus said to Martha:

> *"Did I not say to you that if you would believe you would see the glory of God?"* John 11:40

Jesus was able to say that Lazarus was not dead, because He heard His Father say it. Then He walked into the frame provided and thus completed the picture by speaking life into the dead man.

When Jesus turned water into wine, it was the first miracle to manifest His glory. Many more would follow. Where Jesus is, there is the potential for miracles.

It is one thing to feel the presence and glory of God in a meeting, and it is quite another thing to have that glory manifested. Miracles make the glory real to us.

The glory is a cloud that hovers over our lives, and in the glory cloud, there is the potential for miracles, revival and harvest. Most Christians are content with the presence of the cloud. They are just happy it is hovering over them. They never think to tap its resources for miracles and harvest.

When a natural cloud hovers over a city, the weather forecasters say, "There is a possibility of rain and thunderstorms today." The presence of the cloud presents those very real possibilities. In the same way, when the glory cloud hovers over us, a sense of expectancy fills us, for we know that anything is possible. Far too many people rest in the fact that the cloud is present, and are content to wait for its manifestation — in rain, revival, miracles or harvest.

Some of these people become discouraged and wonder why the presence of the cloud has not manifested itself. In order for a cloud to produce rain, it is not enough that it be seen and felt. There must be an atmospheric pressure in the air to cause rain. This is a scientific fact in the natural, and it is true in the spiritual as well. The pressure needed is our continued hunger and desperate desire to see the glory. Like Moses, we must cry out to God until the manifestation comes.

Mary was not content with the fact that Jesus was present at the marriage in Cana of Galilee. A miracle was needed, and she sought Him until it was accomplished.

Elijah prophesied that rain would come during a time of extended drought. Then he began to travail before God until he saw a sign, a cloud the size of a man's hand. When he saw it, he said to his servant, "Run." He was just that sure that rain was coming, and it did rain over the dry land. Elijah did not stop pressing in until he saw the manifestation of the glory.

One weekend I was preaching in Brittany in the western part of France. We had many healings and salvations. Among those who were saved was a satanist. On Saturday night I spoke a prophetic word that satanists would be saved in the church if the people would allow God to bring in the cloud of

His glory and to break the power of sin in their lives. The whole church responded to the altar call.

That next morning, during the Sunday morning service, a satanist came in and received salvation and a major deliverance. I had spoken what I heard the Lord say, and the members of the church had walked into the frame God had prepared for them. The result was the miracle of a satanist whom no one had invited coming in and receiving salvation.

After the meeting that day, some of the teenagers invited me to go surfing with them. I had been battling a chest and head cold for several days. It was February, and the water was ice cold. I thought probably I should not go, but the young people told me that there had not been any wind or waves for a week already, so I thought probably none of us could actually surf.

More importantly, the Lord had told me that I was already healed. So I told the young people I would go. "Bring your wet suits by faith," I told them.

After I had made this commitment, everything within me told me that I was out of my mind. But that was precisely the point. I was out of my mind, and I was into the mind of Christ. I felt absolutely no fear.

When we got to the beach, the sun was already getting low in the sky. There were no waves or wind in sight, and it was very cold. Apparently I was off the hook. I was glad, because I still wasn't feeling very well.

Then the Lord reminded me that I was healed — whether I felt like it or not — and He instructed me to do something shocking. He told me to command the waves and wind to rise.

I told the teenagers what the Lord had said, and they looked at me with a puzzled expression. I asked them to agree with me anyway. Half jokingly, they did. Nothing seemed to happen.

Then the Lord told me, "Get your wet suits on and prepare to go surfing. The waves are big."

Although our minds were not in agreement with what God was saying (as usual), we did as we were told. We put on our wet suits, picked up our surfboards, and started swimming for deeper water.

The water was freezing cold, and I began to cough more. Then a most amazing thing happened. Beautiful waves began to form from nowhere, and we were able to enjoy a wonderful time of surfing. The surfing was so good, in fact, that my wife and I decided to stay in town an extra day to do some more surfing. My cold had quickly disappeared in the midst of the frigid water and the enjoyment of surfing.

Those teenagers were ecstatic and spread the news of this miracle all over the region. This opened the door for us to come back and do a much larger evangelistic meeting, with many churches in the region cooperating.

What brought this about? I certainly didn't have a special faith to make waves where there were no waves. But I was willing to obey the spontaneous word of God. This launched us into the glory realm, where miracles commonly take place.

Hebrews records:

> *By faith we understand that the worlds were framed by the word of God.*   Hebrews 11:3

The worlds were framed by His word, and that frame was waiting for us to step into it.

The word of God causes creative miracles to be suspended or framed, and you must walk into the frame to complete the picture. Once God has spoken a word directly to you, you can count on the fact that what He said has been created.

In this particular passage, when it says that *"the worlds were framed by the word of God,"* it is speaking of the spoken word of God, or as we often say, the *rhema* word. A *rhema* word is something specific that God speaks to you in a given moment. It is not like the *logos* Word (written Word) that we learn in the faith realm. The *rhema* word comes to us only in the glory realm.

Peter knew this realm. When he had tried fishing

all night without results, he gave up. Then Jesus challenged him:

> *"Launch out into the deep and let down your nets for a catch."*   Luke 5:4

Peter explained that they had been trying all night long and had caught nothing. Still, he was willing to act upon the Lord's word:

> *"At Your word I will let down the net."*
>   Luke 5:5

Although his human reasoning did not agree, Peter was ready to obey the word of the Lord. What happened next amazed everyone. These were experienced fishermen, but they had never had a catch like the one they were about to pull in. Two boats were filled with fish until they were nearly sinking. What a catch that was!

The moment Jesus spoke, I believe, the frame was created. In that very moment, the fish began to congregate in large numbers. All Peter had to do was walk into the frame. The letting down of the nets activated the miracle.

Peter had no faith for fish. He had tried and failed. He did have faith in Jesus' word, and that is what produced the miracle.

Imagine what would have happened if Peter had refused to launch the net again. After all, he and the other men with him were tired and discouraged. An all-night fishing trip that nets absolutely nothing is no fun. In fact, it is exhausting. If Peter had waited, if he had continued reasoning, if he had relied upon popular opinion, the miracle would have been lost. Delayed obedience is nothing more than rebellion and unbelief.

Peter had learned his lesson well: whatever God says, just do it. That's what won him the victory.

Peter had been among the men on the boat the night they were threatened by a storm at sea, and they had seen Jesus coming to them, walking on the water. Peter immediately wanted to join the Lord, but he was no fool. He knew that he couldn't walk on water, so he didn't leap over the side of the boat immediately. Instead, Peter made a very smart move. He would use his faith to tap into the glory realm. He said to Jesus:

> *"Command me to come to You on the water."*
> Matthew 14:28

Peter knew that if Jesus would give the command, it would be a sure thing. He didn't need to muster enough faith to walk on water. He would use his faith to respond to the spoken word, and then God's faith would take over and accomplish the work. The question is not: Do we have enough faith to do it? The question is: Who is giving the command?

When I commanded those waves to rise, I did not have a special faith for waves. I knew that God was speaking to me and that these were not my own thoughts. Since I have experienced that anything He tells me to do always succeeds, I had no fear.

This is the same secret that turned water into wine. Mary told the servants that day:

"Whatever He says to you, do it."   John 2:5

Those servants didn't have faith enough to turn water into wine, but they did have faith in the Person who was giving the commands. Their faith may have been small, but they had enough to respond to Jesus' instructions. This is why the Word of God tells us that if we can have the faith of a mustard seed, we can move mountains. Even small faith combined with a spontaneous obedience to God's spoken word causes miracles.

When your faith runs out, God's faith takes over. Yours is limited, but you can tap into His unlimited supply. This, by far, is the most important secret of the realm of creative miracles.

In Montreal, when they brought that paralyzed

boy to me for prayer, I was about to pray for him (with my own faith), but the Lord stopped me. He said, "Don't lay hands on him. Take him right now, and begin to walk back and forth with him." I did this with the help of that other evangelist, Luigi.

Then, at a certain point, the Lord instructed me to let the boy walk on his own. When I obeyed, the boy was able to walk for the first time in his life.

Many people had prayed for this boy and even fasted, and what God did was, in part, a result of their prayers. The manifestation of his healing, however, came to fruition only when I spontaneously obeyed the *rhema* word I heard the Lord speak. If I had thought about it more than a moment, I might have hesitated and reasoned that it was not worth taking the risk, and the moment might have passed without fruit.

It was that same day that I prophesied to Luigi that soon he would raise the dead. The moment I spoke it, that situation was created and waiting for him to walk into it. Just a week later, he raised the woman from the dead in a hospital. He had walked into the frame God had prepared for him.

If we can respond to the voice of God before our minds have a chance to fully realize what we are doing, we can see miracles. Our spirits are quicker than our minds. That is why we must do things by the Spirit and not simply by experience or according to what has worked for us in the past. When Jesus did miracles, He often did them in a new way each time.

We like formulas and methods that we can use again and again, but God wants us to depend more on Him at all times. He has said:

> *"Behold, I will do a new thing.*
> *Now it shall spring forth;*
> *Shall you not know it?"*   Isaiah 43:19

> *"I have made you hear new things from this time,*
> *Even hidden things, and you did not know them."*   Isaiah 48:6

Since God is the Creator, His phrase *"Let there be"* still echoes throughout the universe. He is creating and will continue to create in miracles, signs and wonders that have never been recorded anywhere at any time. We cannot say that because we have never heard of something or because we have never seen it before, it is not of God. He is doing new things, so we can expect to see things and hear of things that have never before existed.

When we respond to God's *rhema* word spoken in the glory, things that would have taken many years to accomplish can be done in mere moments.

How is it possible for someone to experience instant and significant weight loss? It can only happen in the glory. Our God is Lord over time, and He can do things now that in the natural should take weeks, months or years. The glory is an accelerator:

> *"They are created now and not from the beginning;*
> *And before this day you have not heard them."*
>   Isaiah 48:7

"They are created now!" What does *now* mean? It means NOW. In an instant, right NOW, God can and will do the impossible. There is no time limit in the glory, for it is the eternal realm.

Some would say, like Solomon, that there is nothing new under the sun. In the glory, which comes from above the sun, there are new things that God wants to bring to the Earth. That is why Jesus told us to pray:

> *"Your will be done*
> *On earth as it is in heaven."*   Matthew 6:10

This next great move of God will far surpass anything we have experienced in the past. The miracles we have seen until now — blind eyes open, skin diseases disappear, limbs grow out, paralyzed people walk, deaf ears open, bald people receive hair, teeth filled and crowned with gold and silver — are only a prelude. These are happening because we have allowed God's glory to work in simplicity in creative miracles, but the best is yet to come.

Some are still praying for God to repeat what He did in previous revivals, but what He wants to do has no blueprint to which we can compare it. He wants to do a new thing, so that we can learn to depend on His Spirit. He will not repeat the showers of the past. He is about to give us the former rain and the latter rain combined, and like never before, we will see the creative handiwork of the Almighty.

4

Spontaneous Giving

*For all who were possessors ...
brought the proceeds of the
things that were sold, and laid
them at the apostles' feet; and
they distributed to each as
anyone had need.*

Acts 4:34-35

When I suspended the revival in
Paris after six months of meetings
and much fruitfulness, it was because the Lord told me He wanted
to take us to a new level. He wanted
to restore the emphasis on signs and
wonders common in the early

Church. This, He showed me, would accelerate His work in these last days. As I said, He told me that He would reveal to me three new signs that would be used in this next revival.

As the new signs and wonders of gold dust and gold teeth (along with other creative miracles) became more and more common in our meetings and in gatherings around the world, I began to seek God concerning the third sign of which He had spoken. What I received was a shocking revelation that totally changed my life.

What we seek is usually what we find, especially if we are seeking after what God has promised us. The believers of the first century sometimes became desperate in their search for God. At times, their desperation was driven by serious persecution, such as this case in Acts 4. They prayed fervently:

> *"Now, Lord, look on their threats, and grant to Your servants that with all boldness they may speak Your word, by stretching out Your hand to heal, and that signs and wonders may be done through the name of Your holy Servant Jesus."*
>
> Acts 4:29-30

The disciples were asking God to do healings, signs and wonders because they believed that such signs and wonders would be the most powerful means of validating or confirming what they were preaching. If miracles happened for them, men would know that the Jesus they preached was still alive and still working through them. They wanted boldness to speak the Word of God, and they knew that boldness could come only if they had signs and wonders confirming what they said.

Each new move of the Spirit has a new outpouring of power that comes with it and new manifestations and new truths that are revealed. The outpouring of Pentecost, as recorded in the second chapter of the Book of Acts, was different from the outpouring in the fourth chapter of Acts:

> *And when they had prayed, the place where they were assembled together was shaken; and they were all filled with the Holy Spirit, and they spoke the word of God with boldness.*
>
> Acts 4:31

We go *"from glory to glory,"* and each new glory has a new manifestation. If the apostles had insisted that the experience of the initial Day of Pentecost outpouring (which occurred at the beginning of the Book of Acts) was the only pattern for revival, they never would have progressed. When a move of God's Spirit stops moving, it is no longer a move, and it becomes part of history.

When God moves in a new way, we cannot always compare it to past moves to see if it is of Him. He does new things, so if we are to be pioneers in bringing something new, we must allow God to do things that bypass our current experience.

The New Sign

When God told me there would be three new signs, I was open to them. I saw the gold dust in Ashland and the gold teeth in Vancouver within the same week, and from then on, I was ready for the third sign. It came in a most unexpected manner.

I was attending an anointed conference, and the glory of God again was very strong. I was sure that I would soon see the third manifestation of the glory that God had promised. I don't know what I was expecting, but what I saw was nothing I had anticipated.

As the speaker ministered, suddenly people got up out of their seats and began to surge forward to bless him financially. They put money in his pockets. They left money on the pulpit. They even laid money on the floor at his feet. It was an outpouring of spontaneous giving.

When I saw what was happening, I was reminded of the experience of those first-century believers:

*Now the multitude of those who believed were
of one heart and one soul; neither did anyone
say that any of the things he possessed was his
own, but they had all things in common.*

Acts 4:32

It was then that the amazing giving recorded in
verse 35 began, and the Christians came laying gifts
at the apostles' feet.

I was surprised by the sudden rush to bless the
servant of God I was witnessing, and my mind was
questioning it. The minister was already very blessed
and successful, and I found it hard to believe that
he needed my money. He had a growing television
ministry, and I had my own needs. There were many
things that I wanted to do for God, and they would
all require finances.

At the same time I was having these thoughts, the
Holy Spirit was prompting me to give to the man as
others were doing. I asked, "Lord, why do You want
me to give to this man?"

The Lord told me, "Just do it," and assured me
that He would explain the reasons behind it later.

There was an explosion of God's glory in the place,
and people kept getting up throughout the message
and going forward to give. I was still battling between my mind and the Spirit, but the urging of the
Spirit increased until I decided I should obey God.

My flesh and my human reasoning had won out long enough. After all, this man was reaching many more people with the Gospel than I was. He had not only his meetings and his television ministry, but also his books. I went forward and gave.

Within days of my giving in that meeting, I was invited to speak on three different television programs around the United States. The Lord had been telling us that He would open television to us both here and in Europe, but we had wondered how we could afford it. Now we had it free, and many people were saved and healed through those programs.

In just a week, I was able to reach thousands of people I might otherwise not have reached. When I sowed into the grace and favor another man was experiencing, that same favor came back upon my own life.

When I went back to Europe, television opened to me there as well. People across Europe were blessed by the programs, and this opened new doors to us in many of the European countries. All of this was a result of my spontaneous giving.

This was the same spirit of giving that had possessed the early followers of Christ. As they gave, the power of God was turned on in their lives. Suddenly, they *"had all things in common."* This refers to more than a physical sharing. They all had the same anointing and the same glory.

The men who had accompanied Jesus during His time on the Earth were not the only blessed ones. All of the believers were blessed equally. This resulted in *"great power"* within the Church:

> *And with great power the apostles gave witness to the resurrection of the Lord Jesus. And great grace was upon them all.*   Acts 4:33

With the spirit of spontaneous giving came an explosion of *"great power."* When we sow into the life of a minister or the life of a ministry that has the glory, we get part of that glory back upon our own lives and ministries.

"Great grace was upon them all." What a wonderful testimony! The great grace that the disciples of Jesus experienced after Calvary became common to all believers. I have found that a grace for signs, wonders and miracles comes corporately when the spirit of spontaneous giving erupts in a meeting.

When the early believers began laying money at the feet of the apostles, they were simply responding to the glory of God that rested on the apostles. Paul often spoke of this grace in his letters to the churches, because the members of those churches were partners with him in the Gospel. He said to them:

I have you in my heart, inasmuch as both in my chains and in the defense and confirmation of the gospel, you all are partakers with me of grace. Philippians 1:7

The word *"grace"* is used in relation to ability, anointing, wealth and, especially, glory. Those who supported Paul were to partake of the same level of blessing that was on his life — whether it was in miracles, anointing, favor or finances. The churches Paul planted thus became carriers of the glory that was upon his life.

I learned much about giving at the Pensacola Revival. When we heard about the revival, my wife and I didn't waste any time getting there. We wanted to see what God was doing and partake of it. We were amazed when we saw how people would stand outside the church in line for up to sixteen hours waiting to get into a service. Some even slept outside to get a better place in line for that next evening's meeting. We had never seen anything quite like it before.

In the services, we saw thousands of people running to the altars to receive salvation and freedom from sin. It was very exciting to see them being blessed, and we were also powerfully touched by the revival.

In the very first service we attended, Pastor John

Kilpatrick pulled us out and had the whole congregation pray for us and our ministry in Europe. As they prayed, great tears fell from their eyes, and wailing could be heard throughout the building as the people poured out their hearts to God.

I had Steve Hill and his staff pray for me about ten times during those days. I wanted to take this revival to France, and to other nations of Europe and the world.

Before I left Pensacola, the Lord told me to sow a sizeable offering into the ministry of Steve Hill. I had been reserving the money He spoke to me to give to buy cassette tapes and videos. I had been giving each night in the main offering, and I was sure that some of that would go to Steve. But the more I reasoned, the more the Lord impressed me to sow directly to Steve. I finally obeyed.

When I obeyed God, by sowing into the glory operating in Steve Hill's life, a part of that glory came back upon me. The harvest of that seed resulted in the six-month revival in Paris, which began within weeks of my visit to Pensacola. It was known by some as the Pensacola Revival of France (partly because it began on the same day of the year as did the Revival in Pensacola), but also because God was doing the same things in Paris that He was doing in Pensacola. I had sowed into that glory in Pensacola, and we reaped a measure of the same glory that was upon Steve Hill and the Brownsville Revival. It was amazing.

Perhaps I should not have been surprised. Elisha sowed by serving Elijah, and he was able to receive a double portion of what Elijah had. There is a spiritual principle here: *You reap what you sow.*

I first heard about the gold teeth being manifested in Europe through a minister from Quebec. He had seen over two hundred and fifty teeth filled within four weeks in his ministry in Belgium and in the United States. I later called him and told him that we were just starting to see the same thing but sensed that God wanted to increase these signs upon our ministry for His glory. I asked him to pray for me to receive that same glory so I could use it to see more people touched. He prayed over me.

When I hung up the phone, the Lord told me that it was not "a done deal" yet. He told me to send a check to that man and sow into the glory that was upon his life. Again I questioned the Lord, but He told me, "Just do it." As soon as I obeyed, I saw that grace for gold teeth explode in our meetings. Within two weeks, more than a hundred teeth were filled and crowned in the series of meetings I was doing, and the manifestation continued to grow from there. Spontaneous obedience in giving brings spontaneous miracles of every kind.

I have been greatly blessed since coming in contact with and befriending Ruth Ward Heflin. I received through her ministry an impartation for a new level of glory and a greater release in the area of signs and wonders, revelation and the prophetic. We have seen these new manifestations of glory touch cities and countries that have never experienced such things, and ministering with her has proven to be a blessing many times over. As with the others, God spoke to us to sow into her ministry, and He has sent upon us a measure of the glory so evident in her life.

What does sowing have to do with the glory? Paul explains this in His writings. He says that as a minister sows a spiritual gift to the church, it is the believers' responsibility to respond by sowing materially into that minister's life. Some may have wondered why, after they have had hands laid on them during a revival for a special anointing, they never seem to see that anointing manifested in their lives. It could be because there needs to be a response to that anointing in a physical way. As I once heard my friend Renny McLean say, "Nothing sown, nothing grown."

Some may work with a ministry, as Elisha did, and they will be blessed because of their contribution in that way. The disciples gave up all to follow Jesus, and after He was gone, they walked in the same power He had exhibited. He promised them:

"He who believes in Me, the works that I do he will do also; and greater works than these he will do, because I go to My Father."

John 14:12

"Greater works." Sowing a gift to empower a ministry to do more is a way of sowing to a level of grace on that minister's life and having a measure of it operate in your own life.

Money is only a tool. It enables you to do more. When a ministry has money, it magnifies the ability of that ministry to touch more people. When you give, you help magnify the ability of that ministry, enabling it to do more and reach farther. As a result, you take part of the grace that is upon that ministry. This is not the only way to accomplish it, but it is a key that God is revealing to us today that will unlock a new level of glory.

False Giving

This type of giving should never be confused with what Simon the sorcerer did when he offered money to Peter. Simon wanted to buy the gift of the Holy Spirit. He wanted to manipulate and control the situation.

Simon had earned his living through the spirit of

witchcraft. Now that he was saved, he suddenly found himself unemployed. In those days, when a magician or sorcerer saw another person performing a new trick, he would offer money to buy the secret of it.

Simon was responding in the flesh. As soon as Peter exposed the deception of his heart, Simon dropped the matter.

The difference in the type of spontaneous giving we are talking about is obvious. One is motivated by the flesh, and the other is motivated by the Spirit. When the glory is present, it is often accompanied by a spirit of spontaneous giving. We must learn to obey these promptings of the Holy Spirit and to deny any fleshly motive. Our desire in seeking the glory and the special gifts that come with it must always be to advance the Kingdom of God.

Jesus said:

> *"For everyone to whom much is given, from him much will be required; and to whom much has been committed, of him they will ask the more."* Luke 12:48

We are indeed deeply indebted to God Almighty, and spontaneous giving thus becomes, for us, a pleasure not to be denied.

Spontaneous Giving Releases Resurrection Power

And with great power the apostles gave witness to the RESURRECTION of the Lord Jesus.
Acts 4:33

In Montreal, the gold dust began to fall that first time after a spirit of spontaneous giving had broken out in the meeting while I was still preaching. One lady was led to put her watch on the pulpit. When she broke into tears, I thought it might be because she was sorry she had given. I was wrong. She was weeping with joy because her arm was instantly healed the moment she put her gift on the altar. Within a few minutes, someone had given her a new watch, better than the one she gave.

It was during that same meeting that someone brought me the paralyzed boy to pray for, and when I obeyed the Lord's instructions, the boy was healed. After this miracle occurred, Luigi, the evangelist who had helped me walk the boy around, came up to me and handed me an offering. He told me that he needed to sow into the glory that was working in my life.

The Lord told me to accept the money and to prophesy over Luigi. I prophesied that he would do greater things, and that very soon he would raise the dead. As I said, within a week he had his opportunity. It happened in this way:

He was in the emergency room waiting to have minor surgery to remove a small growth, when someone wheeled in a dead woman and put her on the table he was supposed to occupy. He realized that this was his moment to walk into the prophecy.

He cried out, "Life, come back into her!" and she came back to life, to the amazement of all the doctors present.

Luigi's own surgery went very well that day, but he had much more to rejoice about. He was moving in a new and powerful realm of ministry, and it all started when he had given spontaneously.

There is much more power in sowing financially to someone who is operating on a higher level of glory than there is in just receiving their hands laid upon us. The reason is that we are partnering with them and serving them, so we receive the same rewards and giftings.

The Bible mentions a principle called *"a prophet's reward"* (Matthew 10:42-43). It involves giving to a man or woman of God, as God leads, and receiving a supernatural blessing from that giving. Evangelist Renny McLean tells the story of a woman who attended his meetings. During the meeting, gold dust came down, and there were many miracles. The next day, the woman went to pray for a young boy who had just died at the hospital. Looking at the dead boy, she asked the Lord to manifest the same glory that she had experienced in the meeting the night before. When she had finished praying, she noticed gold dust on the boy, and shortly afterward he opened his eyes. Her simple prayer had resulted in a boy being raised from the dead.

Giving Releases Miracles

Spontaneous giving releases an atmosphere for signs and wonders and miracles and allows a person to partake of a grace working in someone else's ministry. It is a form of serving a ministry.

When a rich woman gave Elisha a room to stay in, and she served him, she was sowing into the glory on his life. Later, Elisha asked her what she wanted. She needed a son, she said, but her husband was very old. Elisha prophesied a son, and the woman conceived and bore a son. This was a result of her obedience to honor the prophet.

When Elisha later heard that the son had died, he returned from Mount Carmel (when it was not yet the season to come to the city). He prayed over the boy, and the boy came back to life.

This same scene was played out in the life of Elijah, Elisha's predecessor. A widow of Zarephath gave him her last meal, and when she did, God performed a miracle for her. She and her son lacked nothing during the remainder of a long drought.

Later, her son died too, and Elijah raised him from the dead. The grace for the raising of the dead was somehow tied into the woman's obedience to give to the prophet carrying the glory.

It should also be noted that Elisha walked in the mantle of Elijah because he served him, thus sowing into his glory for years, just as the disciples had done while following Jesus.

When Mary of Bethany broke an alabaster jar filled with expensive perfume and anointed Jesus with it, she was sowing to the Son of God. He not only had the glory; He was the Source of the glory.

To Judas, what Mary did seemed like a terrible waste. Jesus said, however, that Mary had done this *"for [His] burial"*:

> *"For in pouring this fragrant oil on My body,*
> *she did it for My burial."*   Matthew 26:12

I believe that Mary had caught a revelation of who Jesus was, and as a result, she received Him as her Savior that day. She now wanted to offer something to the Savior.

The gift Mary sowed that day was costly to her.

When we give sacrificially to the Lord as worship, it touches His heart and releases His miracle power.

This was not Mary's first experience in the dynamic of giving to Jesus. She and her siblings had befriended the Lord, and He had gotten in the habit of accepting the hospitality of their home when He was in or near Jerusalem. Although we know that Jesus loved everyone, these three are singled out in the Scriptures as having received a special love from the Lord:

> *Now Jesus loved Martha and her sister [Mary]*
> *and Lazarus.* John 11:5

The ministry of hospitality that Mary, Martha and Lazarus offered to Jesus reminds us of that given to the prophets Elijah and Elisha, and just as those gifts of love were rewarded with miracles of resurrection, Mary was to be rewarded in the same way. Lazarus became ill and died:

> *Now a certain man was sick, Lazarus of*
> *Bethany, the town of Mary and her sister*
> *Martha. IT WAS THAT MARY WHO*
> *ANOINTED THE LORD WITH THE FRA-*
> *GRANT OIL AND WIPED HIS FEET WITH*
> *HER HAIR, WHOSE BROTHER LAZARUS*
> *WAS SICK.* John 11:1-2

Mary had sowed to Jesus' burial and resurrection through her spontaneous and sacrificial gift, and now she would benefit from that same resurrection power:

> *Now when He had said these things, He cried out with a loud voice, "Lazarus, come forth!" And he who had died came out bound hand and foot with graveclothes, and his face was wrapped with a cloth. Jesus said to them, "Loose him, and let him go."* John 11:43-44

This is one of the most memorable stories from the life of Jesus on Earth. He raised Lazarus from the dead.

We have noticed in all of our meetings that when this same spirit of spontaneous giving is working, the atmosphere changes, and the grace for signs, wonders and miracles is usually more prevalent.

In France, for instance, we were believing for a breakthrough in our home church in St. Denis, led by Pastor Robert Baxter. When I was scheduled to preach there one day, the Lord told me to give our pastor my car for a breakthrough. In the middle of my message that day, I handed over the keys and title deed to my car to sow into the glory and release that realm into the church. When I had done this, the people were moved and began to run forward to give spontaneously. As they did, gold dust fell all over the building. To this day, it comes in practically every service, and the finances of the church have been blessed since that time.

In French Guiana, in that jungle area along the Amazon, accessible only by canoe or small airplane, the people began to give spontaneously. It was soon after their spontaneous acts that the gold dust fell in many different colors and we had a great harvest of souls. Many who were involved in witchcraft and some who were members of gangs came forward to give their lives to Christ.

In this acceleration of the glory, in which the Lord is taking us from glory to glory, an acceleration is taking place also in the area of giving.

Sowing Into Good Ground vs Sowing Into Need

When you sow to someone who has the glory, you are definitely sowing into good ground. It is the same ground that Adam and Eve were accustomed to before the fall. The glory was in the garden, and as long as it was there, they did not have to toil and struggle to get their seed to produce a harvest. The earth of the garden was fertile and productive as long as the glory was present. Likewise, when you sow into a ministry that has the glory, you are sowing into that same good ground.

Seed sown into good ground produces a good crop:

> *"But others fell on good ground and yielded a crop: some a hundredfold, some sixty, some thirty.*
> *He who has ears to hear, let him hear!"*
> Matthew 13:8-9

> *"But he who received seed on the good ground is he who hears the word and understands it, who indeed bears fruit and produces: some a hundredfold, some sixty, some thirty."*
> Matthew 13:23

If you sow toward someone who is in need, that is wonderful, and we must do it, but it is not the same thing as sowing into the glory. Giving to the poor or to those in need is different from sowing into the glory.

For example, when the boy with the five loaves and two fish gave his lunch to Jesus, the Lord multiplied it to feed more than five thousand people. If the boy had attempted to give what he had directly to the poor, that would not have been wrong, but he would not have been able to feed very many poor people. Because Jesus had the glory, the food multiplied when it was given to Him. The glory is good ground.

Lending vs Sowing Into the Glory

The Bible says:

> *He who has pity on the poor lends to the LORD,*
> *And He will pay back what he has given.*
>   Proverbs 19:17

When you lend something to someone (like a pencil, for example), you usually get back only what you have lent. Giving to the poor is what you do as a result of the harvest that comes in after giving into the glory. If you gave all to the poor and got back everything you had given, you would still not be able to feed many poor people. If you sow first to ministries that have the glory, what you have sown will come back multiplied many times over. Then you have much more to give to the poor and to those in need out of your harvest.

Why should we give to the ministry of a man or woman who is already financially blessed? Let us look at what the queen of Sheba did:

> *Now when the queen of Sheba heard of the fame*
> *of Solomon concerning the name of the LORD,*
> *she came to test him with hard questions. She*
> *came to Jerusalem with a very great retinue,*
> *with camels that bore spices, very much gold,*

and precious stones; and when she came to Solomon, she spoke with him about all that was in her heart.

Then she gave the king one hundred and twenty talents of gold, spices in great quantity, and precious stones. There never again came such abundance of spices as the queen of Sheba gave to King Solomon. 1 Kings 10:1-2 and 10

Why would anyone give such a large amount to a man who was already considered to be the richest person in the world? It was because the glory of God was on Solomon's life and kingdom. The queen of Sheba was in need of the wisdom, revelation, glory and riches Solomon had to share with her nation, and this was her way of getting it.

Her sacrifice proved to be wise. She left for home with more than she had when she had arrived:

Now King Solomon gave the queen of Sheba all she desired, whatever she asked, besides what Solomon had given her according to the royal generosity. So she turned and went to her own country, she and her servants.

1 Kings 10:13

The queen of Sheba sowed into the glory and received a portion of that glory for herself and her nation. The financial blessing she received was in addition to the spiritual blessing she had received by being associated with God's people.

Whoever Blessed Abraham Would Be Blessed

Abraham became the father of many nations, and God promised him great blessings. He also told him:

> *"I will bless those who bless you,*
> *And I will curse him who curses you;*
> *And in you all the families of the earth shall be*
> *blessed."*   Genesis 12:3

Because the blessing and glory of God was upon Abraham's life, whoever blessed him and his descendants would be blessed. This is a biblical rule.

Ministries that have the glory are surprisingly blessed on all sides. If we can stay long enough in the glory, physical needs will become less and less of a problem.

Eliminating the Time Limit

The Bible says that as long as the Earth remains, there will be seedtime and harvest time:

> *"While the earth remains,*
> *Seedtime and harvest,*

Cold and heat,
Winter and summer,
And day and night
Shall not cease."　　　　Genesis 8:22

When we sow into the glory, we are not sowing into the earthly realm, where there is *"seedtime"* and *"harvest."* The element of time is removed or diminished in the glory. If we were to go to Heaven with a cancer, the second we got there, the cancer would be gone. In this same way, seedtime and harvest often become the same when we sow into the glory. We reap instantly.

In Heaven there is no time as we know it. That is why, when people sow into the glory, new money miracles take place almost simultaneously. Money begins to multiply in the pockets, purses and wallets of the people right then and there.

Such miracles should not surprise us. Elijah, Elisha and Jesus all started and ended their ministries with miracles of provision. The fact that we are seeing some of the same type of miracle is a sign that we are coming into that same anointing.

Money Miracles

In Ireland, a conference where I preached was short a large amount of money. Some of those who had registered cancelled, but the hotel made the leaders pay anyway. Toward the end of the conference, the men came to me and explained to me the problem. They were not sure they would be able to give me an offering for my services. I told them not to worry about it, to do whatever they needed to do. I didn't want to see them indebted by the meeting.

When the final offering was about to be taken, the leader of the conference was instructed by the Lord to receive the offering for me, not for the needs of the conference. In this way, they would be sowing into the glory they had experienced in our ministry.

At first, I was reluctant to accept it, remembering their plight. I agreed when I sensed that God was at work. The next day, when the accountant who was handling the funds of the conference counted the money one more time, it had multiplied. With that miracle, they more than covered their loss, and they had funds left over for the next conference.

In Israel, several people received money miracles in our meetings. Some had the money in their purses multiply after giving.

I prophesied that a miracle would be done for the congregation after I left the building. Within minutes after I left, several policemen walked in carrying an expensive sound system that had been stolen from the congregation a year earlier. Since the pastor had never reported it stolen, he wondered how the police knew whom to return it to. The officers said the thief had felt convicted and had turned the sound system over to them, telling them where he had stolen it so they could return it. What a miracle!

A few days later, the pastors gave us free tickets to fly business class on Suisse Air anywhere in Europe. They had accumulated some extra travel miles and could have used the tickets themselves, but they decided to bless us instead. Since we often travel in Europe, it proved to be a great blessing.

My wife and I prayed that the pastor and his wife would receive a miracle blessing for having given the tickets. Within a few days after we had left Israel, they called and told us that someone had given them twenty thousand dollars.

During that week of giving, the congregation also received a van, and someone was led to pay an entire month's rent for the congregation and to pay the salary of someone to run the food and clothing distribution ministry of the congregation.

A few weeks later, the pastor went to the bank to deposit 400 shekels. When he counted it, he had 1,000 shekels. He counted again and had 1,400 shekels. He counted it one last time, and it had multiplied to 1,800 shekels.

All of this happened to a young congregation because of the spirit of spontaneous giving that came upon the members.

Obedience Is the Key

Whatever God says to you to do, just do it. If He is speaking, what He is saying is coming from the glory. When you respond spontaneously to the glory, instant miracles take place. When you sow into or in response to the glory, financial miracles can occur in a short span of time and even instantly — since there is no time in the glory. Also, since the glory is good ground, what you have given will be multiplied back to you thirty, sixty and a hundred times over. How can you lose?

5

A Revival of Wisdom

And men of all nations, from all the kings of the earth who had heard of his wisdom, came to hear the wisdom of Solomon.
1 Kings 4:34

With this new wave of signs and wonders, the Lord is releasing a new wave of wisdom, revelation and knowledge. These are keys that allow us to venture into the untapped realms of glory in this new move of God, and as the miracles increase, so will the anointing of supernatural wisdom. This phenomenon will eventually become so powerful that people will come from all over the world just to hear the wisdom of God expressed, as they did in Solomon's day.

Through His prophet Habakkuk, God said:

> *"For the earth will be filled*
> *With the knowledge of the glory of the* LORD,
> *As the waters cover the sea."*

Habakkuk 2:14

This verse is often misquoted. We say that the Earth will be filled with the glory of the Lord, rather than with the KNOWLEDGE of the glory of the Lord. It is one thing to sense the glory in a meeting, and it is quite another thing to have the *knowledge* of that glory. When we have the knowledge, we not only sense the glory, but we have the key to releasing miracles and manifestations from that glory.

Some may have wondered why at times they have sensed the glory, and yet they have never seen a physical manifestation of that glory. Having the knowledge of the glory makes the difference.

The glory could be likened to a cloud hovering over a city. The people see the cloud, but they lack the knowledge or wisdom necessary to make it rain. Clouds come and go sometimes without yielding rain. Now God is revealing to us the keys to releasing spiritual rain from the clouds of glory.

The apostle Paul knew the mysteries of revelation more than most men of his time, and this allowed him to tap into realms other men only dreamed of. It was this gift that enabled Paul to write more than half of the New Testament. He also walked in unusual miracles, he saw the third heaven opened, and he received multitudes of other victories. Fortunately, Paul passed along some of these keys to us in his writings.

In Paul's prayer for the Ephesian believers, for instance, we find his sentiments in this regard:

> ... *making mention of you in my prayers: that the God of our Lord Jesus Christ, the Father of glory, may give to you the spirit of wisdom and revelation in the knowledge of Him.*
> Ephesians 1:16-17

"Wisdom," "revelation" and "knowledge" are keys that open the door to greater things in God. When we use these keys, we can expect to receive what lies behind the door:

> ... *the eyes of your understanding being enlightened; that you may know what is the hope of His calling.*   Ephesians 1:18

Once you grasp a revelation of your calling in

Him, then you can fully enter through its doorway
with knowledge and wisdom. This is essential to
walk into the frame that God has already prepared
for your life.

Supernatural Wisdom
Unlocks Heaven's Supplies

*... what are the riches of the glory of His inher-
itance in the saints.*   Ephesians 1:18

We know that in Heaven there is no lack. We also
know, from these and other scriptures, that we have
an inheritance in Heaven. For instance, we will have
perfect bodies when we get to Heaven, where there
is no sickness. Since the Lord told us to pray, *"Your
will be done on Earth as it is in Heaven,"* this means
that God can bring heavenly things to us here on
the Earth.

When the same glory that is in Heaven comes
down to the Earth, supernatural provision comes,
and you can tap into your inheritance. Once you
truly have a revelation that there is more than
enough reserved for you in Heaven, you will no
longer walk in lack — as long as you stay in the
glory. This is why Jesus said:

"Do not lay up for yourselves treasures on

> *earth, where moth and rust destroy and where*
> *thieves break in and steal; but lay up for your-*
> *selves treasures in heaven, where neither moth*
> *nor rust destroys and where thieves do not break*
> *in and steal. For where your treasure is, there*
> *your heart will be also."* Matthew 6:19-21

If you can bring the glory of Heaven to the Earth, then the treasures of Heaven will be manifested upon the Earth. Just as gold dust has been falling from Heaven as a result of the glory, so other heavenly things can come to us.

This is one of the reasons we have been experiencing new types of financial miracles, like money mysteriously appearing in people's wallets or purses. It often happens right after they have sown into the glory. God is showing us that Heaven has no lack.

Once we have this revelation, laying up treasure on Earth becomes a much more risky proposition. If we lay up treasure in Heaven, we can make withdrawals from it whenever we get into the glory. When we do, we will find that it has multiplied — thirty-, sixty- and a hundredfold. This is the best banking system in the world, and we don't even need an ATM card to access it.

In one of our services, the people came to the front to give spontaneously, but a man from Kenya had nothing to give. He told the Lord this, and the Lord said to him, "I give seed to the sower." Then the Lord told him to look in his wallet. There he found money that had not been there before. He went forward to give the money, and then he came to the microphone and testified about this miracle.

In this case, it was not a large amount, but God is doing financial miracles for His people that are quite large, involving thousands and even millions of dollars. As we have seen, Paul wrote:

> *For we are His workmanship, created in Christ Jesus for good works, which God prepared beforehand that we should walk in them.*
>
> Ephesians 2:10

The key to *"walk[ing] in them,"* once you are in the glory, is through revelation and knowledge. If we don't know (through revelation) that something exists, we cannot walk in it. If no one told us that we had inherited a million dollars from a long-lost relative, we would not know where to go to claim it or even that we could. It is the same in the Spirit. Once we get the revelation that we actually have a great inheritance laid up for us (added to what we have been sowing into Heaven), then we can begin to unlock what has already been reserved for us — through the golden keys of revelation and wisdom in the glory.

Solomon said:

For wisdom is a defense as money is a defense.
Ecclesiastes 7:12

Happy is the man who finds wisdom,
And the man who gains understanding;
For her proceeds are better than the profits of
silver,
And her gain than fine gold.
She is more precious than rubies,
And all the things you may desire cannot be
compared with her. Proverbs 3:13-15

Why is wisdom greater than *"profits"* and greater than *"all the things you may desire,"* meaning anything you could possibly want? Because if you have wisdom, you will have profits and anything else you need.

Many people think that the Bible instructs us not to have riches, but this is not true. It admonishes us not to seek gold and silver, but rather wisdom, so that we can tap into all the available riches for God's Kingdom. This is why the apostle Paul prayed for wisdom for the Ephesians. It is the key that allows us to tap into all the other dimensions of our inheritance.

When you are in need, don't just ask God to meet

that specific need. Ask for wisdom, and you will know what to do to unlock more blessings.

When presented with a choice, Solomon asked for wisdom from God. He knew the secret that with wisdom comes material blessing:

> *Length of days is in her [wisdom's] right hand,*
> *In her left hand riches and honor.*
>
> Proverbs 3:16

When Solomon asked for wisdom instead of gold and silver, fame and power, God gave him everything he lacked. He became the richest and most powerful man of his time. He was also known as the wisest, and as we have seen, men came from many places just to witness his great wisdom. It was the wisdom that unlocked the rest of what Solomon needed.

How did such extraordinary wisdom come to Solomon? It did not come as simply as some might imagine. Before God made the offer to Solomon that resulted in his receiving extraordinary wisdom, he did something that began the entire process:

> *Now the king went to Gibeon to sacrifice there,*
> *for that was the great high place: Solomon of-*
> *fered a thousand burnt offerings on that altar.*
>
> 1 Kings 3:4

This very expensive offering made by Solomon was the thing that started his rise to wisdom and success. He sowed directly into the glory, using what little wisdom he had to bless God. This unlocked all of Heaven's resources.

God's response to this gift was sure:

> At Gibeon the LORD appeared to Solomon in a dream by night; and God said, "Ask! What shall I give you?"   1 Kings 3:5

Solomon was careful with his reply. He was very young to be a king, and he desperately needed wisdom to rule Israel. He could have asked for anything, but he asked for wisdom, and that gave him access to everything else. He prayed:

> "Therefore give to Your servant an understanding heart to judge Your people, that I may discern between good and evil. For who is able to judge this great people of Yours?" The speech pleased the LORD, that Solomon had asked this thing.   1 Kings 3:9-10

When *your* prayers please the Lord, great favor will be shown to you, as it was to Solomon.

One of the lessons we learn from Solomon is that he did not pray flippantly, but showed the same (if not more) respect in God's presence as we would have if meeting an earthly president or king. Because of this, God was ready to bless him:

> *Then God said to him: "Because you have asked this thing, and have not asked long life for yourself, nor have asked riches for yourself, nor have asked the life of your enemies, but have asked for yourself understanding to discern justice, behold, I have done according to your words; see, I have given you a wise and understanding heart ... . And I have also given you what you have not asked: both riches and honor, so that there shall not be anyone like you among the kings all your days."*   1 Kings 3:11-13

Asking God for an anointing of wisdom pleases Him and may result in a special revival of supernatural wisdom. This is clearly what happened with Solomon, and *"men of all nations"* heard of his wisdom and traveled to Jerusalem to witness it personally.

Supernatural Wisdom Looses Miracles

Paul prayed for wisdom for the Ephesians because he knew that this gift unlocks new realms of the glory:

> *... and WHAT IS THE EXCEEDING GREAT-
> NESS OF HIS POWER TOWARD US WHO
> BELIEVE, ACCORDING TO THE WORK-
> ING OF HIS MIGHTY POWER.*
>
> Ephesians 1:19

Another realm that wisdom unlocks is the realm of miracles. What does this phrase *"according to the working of His mighty power"* really mean to us? God is not only turning up the power and increasing the glory, but He is giving us the knowledge of His glory. He is teaching us the inner workings of His mighty power. He is giving us keys that will unleash the greatest miracles ever recorded.

What does wisdom have to do with miracles? Everything! Wisdom and revelation knowledge are the keys to the miracle realm.

Once, when I was praying for a boy with a paralyzed arm, the Lord told me to sing the prayer. As I sang, the glory began to come, and the boy was instantly healed.

In the case of the boy in the wheelchair, I was asked to lay hands on him. But when I asked God for wisdom to know what to do, He told me not to lay hands on him and showed me exactly what to do. At first, nothing seemed to be happening, but by the time the Lord told us to let him go and tell him to walk by himself, he was able to start walking.

When Renny McLean was asked to pray for a retarded boy, he asked the Lord what to do. The Lord told him to make the boy run with him. He could not see how running could heal the boy's mind, but he decided to obey and not try to figure it out. The wisdom of God is greater than our human reasoning. As he ran with the boy, the boy's mind was healed.

Later, God explained the principle behind this act. Before a person acts, he must think. In this case, however, God made the boy act first, and then his mind caught up with his action.

The key was simply listening to the wisdom or revelation of God and obeying it instantly — whether or not it made sense at the time.

Jesus moved in miracle power through wisdom:

> *And when the Sabbath had come, He began to teach in the synagogue. And many hearing Him were astonished, saying, "Where did this Man get these things? AND WHAT WISDOM IS THIS WHICH IS GIVEN TO HIM, THAT SUCH MIGHTY WORKS ARE PERFORMED BY HIS HANDS."*   Mark 6:2

> *"Where did this Man get this wisdom and these mighty works?"*   Matthew 13:54

When Jesus performed miracles, people noticed that He possessed great wisdom. There has always been a direct connection between wisdom and miracles.

The apostle Paul moved in great miracles:

> *Now God worked unusual miracles by the hands of Paul, so that even handkerchiefs or aprons were brought from his body to the sick, and the diseases left them and the evil spirits went out of them.* Acts 19:11-12

Paul had seized upon the revelation that all he needed was a point of contact to release the power of God upon the sick and suffering. He knew that if he was limited to the laying on of hands, he could not reach everyone. He therefore used aprons or prayer cloths to release the power of God and reach out to people he could not personally visit for miracles, healings and deliverances.

Thanks to that revelation, we now know that people can be healed when we pray for them over the telephone, or even when they are watching a minister on television.

Benny Hinn has often told the people watching his program to lay hands on their television sets to receive healing. Somewhere along the line, he received the revelation that all the people needed was a point of contact to release their faith. He does not have to personally lay hands on them or call them out during one of his crusades in order for them to be healed.

During that six-month revival in Paris, as I have said, we used prayer cloths to reach people who couldn't come to the meetings. Many were healed of cancer, leukemia and other sicknesses through prayer cloths, and some of them were on the other side of the world.

Some even put these cloths under the pillows of mentally tormented people, and they were freed. Women put them under the pillows of their unsaved husbands, and the conviction of the Holy Spirit worked on them all through the night. One simple revelation can revolutionize an entire move of God.

Stephen, the martyr, moved in great miracles, and he also had an unusual gift of wisdom. *"They were not able to resist [his] wisdom"*:

> *And Stephen, full of faith and power, did great*
> *wonders and signs among the people.*
> *And they were not able to resist the wisdom*
> *and the Spirit by which he spoke.*
>
> Acts 6:8 and 10

God used Moses to perform some of the greatest miracles, signs and wonders ever recorded, and he was also a man *"learned in all wisdom"*:

> *And Moses was learned in all the wisdom of*
> *the Egyptians, and was mighty in words and*
> *deeds.*   Acts 7:22

We know that true wisdom comes from God and that worldly wisdom is only a perverted reflection of the true thing. Here again, however, we see a connection between wisdom and the miracle-working power of God.

Daniel moved in remarkable wisdom, and he also displayed the power of God to the Babylonians:

> *And in all matters of wisdom and understand-*
> *ing about which the king examined them, he*
> *found them ten times better than all the magi-*
> *cians and astrologers who were in all his realm.*
>   Daniel 1:20

Again we find a direct connection between wisdom and moving in miracles and the supernatural. Daniel's wisdom surpassed that of the sorcerers of his day. Their wisdom failed the critical test:

> *Then the king gave the command to call the*
> *magicians, the astrologers, the sorcerers, and*
> *the Chaldeans to tell the king his dreams.*
>   Daniel 2:2

It is interesting to note that even in Bible days, those who moved in the supernatural — whether they were on God's side or not — were often called *"wise men,"* as these men in Babylon were (Daniel 2:12-14). Why would magicians, astrologers, sorcerers and the like be called *"wise men"*? It was because the people of that day recognized a direct connection between wisdom and miraculous powers.

Satan's wisdom is always limited, and these so-called *"wise men"* could not interpret the king's dream. This angered the king, and he ordered them to be executed. Their lives were spared only because Daniel had the wisdom to interpret the dream:

> *Therefore Daniel went to Arioch, whom the king had appointed to destroy the wise men of Babylon. He went and said thus to him: "Do not destroy the wise men of Babylon; take me before the king, and I will tell the king the interpretation."*   Daniel 2:24

> *Then the secret was revealed to Daniel in a night vision. So Daniel blessed the God of heaven.*
> *Daniel answered and said:*
> *"Blessed be the name of God forever and ever,*
> *For wisdom and might are His. ...*
> *He gives wisdom to the wise*

> *And knowledge to those who have under-*
> *standing.*
> *He reveals deep and secret things."*
>
> Daniel 2:19-22

When the Lord spoke the worlds into being, wisdom was there with Him, and was the tool He used to bring about the first creative miracles ever recorded:

> *The LORD by wisdom founded the earth;*
> *By understanding He established the heavens;*
> *By His knowledge the depths were broken up,*
> *And clouds drop down the dew.*
>
> Proverbs 3:19-20

The same tool of wisdom, used by God when creating the heavens and the Earth, is available to us today.

Wisdom, understanding and knowledge were actually created before the Earth was created. Wisdom was (and still is) the tool God used to perform creative miracles:

> *The LORD possessed me at the beginning of His*
> *way,*
> *Before His works of old.*
> *I have been established from everlasting,*

From the beginning, before there was ever an earth.

While as yet He had not made the earth or the fields,

Or the primal dust of the world.

When He prepared the heavens, I was there.
                    Proverbs 8:22 and 26-27

   In the beginning God created the heavens and the Earth, but before the beginning He created wisdom. Wisdom was His servant working behind the scenes:

   Then I was beside Him as a master craftsman;
   And I was daily His delight.   Proverbs 8:30

   He has made the earth by His power,
   He has established the world by His wisdom.
                    Jeremiah 10:12

   Ask God for the spirit of wisdom so that you can tap into the power of creative miracles. Then thank Him for this priceless gift with a prayer of thankfulness, as did Daniel:

   "I thank You and praise You,
   O God of my fathers;
   You have given me wisdom and might,
   And have now made known to me what we asked of You."   Daniel 2:23

Supernatural Wisdom Raises the Dead

> *... the Father of glory, may give to you the spirit of wisdom and revelation in the knowledge of Him.*
>
> *... which He worked in Christ when He raised Him from the dead.*
>
> Ephesians 1:17 and 20

In the summer of 1999, when I was preaching the final night of a series of meetings in Montreal, Canada, in the church pastored by Pierre Cyr, something exciting happened. A spirit of revelation and wisdom came upon me in the middle of the sermon. Although I did not have time to search out doctrinally what God was showing me, He told me to share it.

I was preaching about Ezekiel in the valley of dry bones. God had told him to raise those bones up by the spoken word. As we have seen in earlier chapters, when you say what God is saying, something happens. Ezekiel was commanded to do this, and he was promised that his words would bring life. He was told to say:

> *"Thus says the Lord* God *to these bones: 'Surely I will cause breath to enter into you, and you shall live.' "*   Ezekiel 37:5

The moment Ezekiel said what God said, something began to happen:

> *So I prophesied as I was commanded; and as I prophesied, there was a noise, and suddenly a rattling; and the bones came together, bone to bone.*   Ezekiel 37:7

As I was speaking in Montreal, I suddenly saw something very clearly. It seemed so simple that I wondered why I had never seen it before. The next verse said:

> *Indeed, as I looked, the sinews and the flesh came upon them, and the skin covered them over; but there was no breath in them.*
>
> Ezekiel 37:8

I suddenly realized how the dead were raised. I was reading from the French Bible, and it used the word *"spirit"* instead of the word *"breath."* The same Hebrew word was being translated two slightly different ways.

The bones of these dead people were now covered with flesh, but they were still dead. The reason this was true is explained in this verse. *"There was no spirit in them."* Once a person dies, his human spirit (that God has given to each person) departs into Heaven or Hell. The only way a dead body can rise again is if the spirit of that person comes back into his body. With that in mind, now look at the next verses:

> *Also He said to me, "Prophesy to the breath [spirit], prophesy, son of man, and say to the breath [spirit], 'Thus says the Lord GOD: "Come from the four winds, O breath [spirit], and breathe on these slain, that they may live." ' "*
> *So I prophesied as He commanded me, and breath [spirit] came into them, and they lived, and stood upon their feet, an exceedingly great army.* Ezekiel 37:9-10

Having the knowledge of how spiritual things work helps greatly when it comes time to obey God in such a case. All we need to do when God tells us to raise a dead person is make sure that the human spirit of that person comes back into the dead body. This done, the person will live again. It is because the spirit of a person is the real person (that lives eternally), not the flesh.

It was after sharing this revelation that I prophesied over Luigi that he would raise the dead. Armed with this revelation, he did it just a week later.

When he saw his opportunity, he shouted out to the corpse, "Spirit of life, come into her!" At that moment, the woman opened her eyes and returned to life.

The first account of resurrection power in the Bible was found in the garden shortly after God created the Earth:

> *And the LORD God formed man of the dust of the ground, and breathed into his nostrils the breath [spirit] of life; and man became a living being.*   Genesis 2:7

Even though man had been formed, he needed one more ingredient — a spirit. Life is in the spirit. God then breathed a portion of Himself into man, and man lived.

Elisha walked in this same wisdom and revelation glory, and he also raised the dead:

> *When Elisha came into the house, there was the child, lying dead on his bed. He went in therefore, shut the door behind the two of them, and prayed to the LORD. And he went up and lay on the child, AND PUT HIS MOUTH ON HIS MOUTH, his eyes on his eyes, and his hands on his hands; and he stretched himself out on the child, and the flesh of the child became warm.*   2 Kings 4:32-34

I believe that when Elisha put his mouth on the mouth of the child, he literally breathed into the boy. We see in the previous verse that he had sent his servant Gehazi and told him to put his staff on the face of the child, but this did not produce the desired effect. When the prophet himself came and stretched himself out upon the child, the breath, or spirit, of the boy came back into him. This was symbolic of the way in which God created us in His image.

Elisha stayed in the glory until the work was complete:

> *He returned and walked back and forth in the house, and again went up and stretched himself out on him; then the child sneezed seven times, and the child opened his eyes.*
>
> 2 Kings 4:35

There is a principle here. In emergency situations, when someone has passed out, his spirit is beginning to leave him. When this happens, there is a rather common technique now used called "mouth-to-mouth resuscitation." This word *resuscitation* comes from the same root word as *resurrection*. Mouth-to-mouth resuscitation works, even reviving some who have already died or who are in the process of dying. God seems to honor this prophetic act, even when it is done by unbelievers.

This is not to say that we should all breathe into dead people and expect to see every one of them raised up. It is simply a prophetic sign which gives us an understanding of how things work in the Spirit.

I am convinced that in the days ahead the raising of the dead to life again will be one of the most common manifestations marking the last-day move of God. The Lord has shown me that whole groups of people will even be raised from the dead as a simple servant of the Lord commands breath to come back into them.

These dead perhaps will have died through war, disease, terrorist attacks or natural disasters, but that's not the important thing. What is important is that God is empowering His people with wisdom to raise the dead. Very soon now the raising of the dead will even be caught on television as a sign to the world of the power of our God. We are entering the last days, the Elijah/Jesus dispensation.

When the glory comes, ask God to manifest His glory in the raising of the dead. Listen for revelation and wisdom that He may whisper into your ear. The raising of the dead is the glory of God manifested, as it was with the raising of Jesus' friend Lazarus:

> *When Jesus heard that, He said, "This sickness is not unto death, but for THE GLORY OF GOD, that the Son of man may be glorified through it."*
> *Jesus said to her, "Did I not say to you that if you would believe you would see THE GLORY OF GOD?"*   John 11:4 and 40

Part of seeing the glory of God, therefore, is seeing the dead among us raised to life. Jesus gave us the example, when He raised Lazarus from the dead, but we can still see these same miracles today.

Supernatural Wisdom Releases Authority

> *... and seated Him at His right hand in the heavenly places, far above all principality and power and might and dominion, and every name that is named, not only in this age but also in that which is to come. And He put all things under His feet, and gave Him to be head over all things to the church.*   Ephesians 1:20-22

Authority comes from a supernatural revelation. God is giving us revelation concerning our speaking to those in authority in the world in any and every sphere of influence. Just as the apostles and prophets of old stood before world rulers, so God is putting upon us the burden and revelation to speak to the kings and rulers of this world as a testimony before the end. As the glory increases, the favor of God will come on many for these crucially important tasks.

As we have seen, Isaiah foretold:

> *Arise, shine;*
> *For your light has come!*
> *And the glory of the* Lord *is risen upon you.*
> *The Gentiles shall come to your light,*
> *And kings to the brightness of your rising.*
>
> Isaiah 60:1 and 3

Jesus walked in this authority. When He was just beginning His ministry and the men of Nazareth wanted to throw Him off a cliff, He escaped into the crowd. They could not take Him before His time. He knew that the authority He had from His Father was greater than any authority of man.

Later, the disciples would escape when they were imprisoned and continue to do the will of the Lord until their time had come. I believe that we should more often exercise our God-given authority, and when we have a revelation of who we are in Christ, we can.

An airline employee gave me a ticket to fly to a conference in Dallas (where I was also to have a television interview). When I checked in at the ticket counter, the agent entered the information into the computer and then told me that the ticket I had was not valid. The employee who gave it to me had apparently changed departments, she said. I asked her to check again because I had just talked to my friend, and he had told me it was good. She insisted that it was not.

I went to the back of the line to ponder what I should do next. The flight would be leaving soon. "What should I do, Lord?" I prayed.

The Lord told me to take the flight, so I went back to the counter and asked the woman to please check again. She became a little irritated, told me that I shouldn't even have that ticket in my possession, and asked me to return it to her.

I went back to where I had left my bags to get the ticket, and as I did, I again asked the Lord what I should do. He said to me, "I told you to take the plane, not to ask a second opinion. This is My airport, and you are My ambassador. Go on up, and take the flight."

With my ticket in hand, I quickly made my way to the departure gate. At the gate, the same thing happened. The agent typed my information into the computer, and then she said, "I see that you already started to check in downstairs. Your ticket is invalid. What are you doing here?"

I answered that I really needed to take this flight and that there must have been a mistake. She proceeded to call the lady downstairs, and I began to pray for the favor of God and to declare: *"The Kingdom of Heaven is at hand."* I was thinking of Jesus' command to the disciples:

> *"And as you go, preach, saying, 'The kingdom of Heaven is at hand.' Heal the sick, cleanse the lepers, raise the dead, cast out demons. Freely you have received, freely give."*
>
> Matthew 10:7-8

There was a very obvious connection between the declaration of the Kingdom of Heaven and seeing the power of God displayed in mighty miracles. I was believing God to overrule the airline's decision and to get me on that flight.

Suddenly the agent changed her mind and hung up. "Oh," she said, "it's probably one of those lazy workers sending us more work up here." Then she gave me my boarding passes, coming and going. I had a great time in the conference in Dallas and in the television interview on Channel 55 with Marcus and Joni Lamb.

Immediately after the interview, I went to see my father before flying back to Phoenix. A recently certified doctor of alphabiotics, he was adjusting people's necks and backs, something that he does on the side in a health food store. The Lord told me to pray for the people he was working on. I asked him if it would be all right, and he agreed. I began to tell the people, "Jesus is going to heal you."

"Is this a new technique?" they asked. I told them it was.

As I prayed for people, legs grew and backs and necks popped into place. The shoppers in the store were in awe of what God was doing, and many stepped out of the line to buy their health food products and got in line for an adjustment. The glory of God suddenly electrified the store.

The owners also came over to see what was happening. At first, I thought they would stop me, but they seemed to be frozen with surprise, their mouths open. The Lord whispered to me, *"The Kingdom of Heaven is at hand."* I felt total freedom, as if I were in one of my own meetings.

After the people got free adjustments from Jesus, I began to minister to them spiritually. A German stewardess involved in the New Age movement received the Lord as her Savior.

I approached the cashier and began to prophesy to her, revealing things in her past that God wanted to mend. She wept loudly.

The glory filled that place, and it was an awesome experience. It was not so much the fact that there were a few miraculous healings, but rather that the Kingdom, or government, of God had taken over the place — because of the glory of the Lord. It happened because I received a revelation from God of my authority in Him.

The Bible shows us that we are seated with Christ in heavenly places (see Ephesians 2:6). Since there is no distance in the glory, we are as near to Heaven as we are to anything here on Earth. When we are in the glory, and we speak to people, we are speaking from the position where Christ has seated us in heavenly places. Therefore, people will recognize our authority. If we speak only from our position here on the Earth (without the glory), our words cannot carry the same weight. The glory represents the weight of God's authority, and kings and others in authority recognize authority when they see it.

This same glory took the simple fisherman Peter and made him into an ambassador for the King of kings. From then on, people of great worldly authority recognized Peter's heavenly authority.

When Peter denied Jesus, he no longer walked in that same authority, and he feared even a simple woman who questioned him. On the Day of Pentecost, after the Holy Spirit had fully come, Peter preached to the very people he had feared only days before. The difference was that he had been touched by a new dimension of glory and had recovered his heavenly authority.

In the realm of authority, everything is done by revelation and wisdom. Once you get a revelation of your seat in the heavenly places and you walk in that glory, it is no longer you speaking, but Christ in you. All authority stems from revelation in the glory, and we are experiencing a revival of that holy wisdom.

Paul, who was writing the letter to the Ephesians, knew this authority well. He spoke to religious and governmental leaders with great authority. When he was a prisoner on a ship, and the Lord showed him that the ship was about to be wrecked, he still had his authority. He told the captain of the ship what God's instructions were to save the people on board.

When Paul made it safely to an island, everyone on the island was healed, including the governor of the island. The Gospel was preached on that island through this prisoner.

Paul spent time in chains, but this did not diminish his authority. He called himself an ambassador in chains and still continued to lead the churches in his apostolic authority. He did not even fear Nero, the leader of the Roman Empire, who could have had him killed on any whim. Paul said:

For to me, to live is Christ, and to die is gain.
But if I live on in the flesh, this will mean fruit
from my labor; yet what I shall choose I cannot
tell.   Philippians 1:21-22

Paul had the authority to choose; therefore he did not fear the authority of Nero. He knew that his release, death or imprisonment was a decision between him and God.

Basically, Paul was saying, "God and I are working on this decision of whether I should stay or go. Once we have made up our minds, Nero, we will let you know what you are allowed to do with me." Until then, the apostle continued his writing ministry from prison. That is the power of the authority that comes with supernatural wisdom.

Jesus walked in this same authority when He was threatened and mocked. He knew that the only authority his accusers had was the authority His Father had given them.

When Paul and Silas were in prison, they began to worship the Lord. As they did, the glory came in and shook the place. The Kingdom of the Lord took priority over the authority of the Roman Empire, the guard and his family received the Lord, and Paul and Silas went on their way preaching to others.

Jesus told the disciples to declare that the Kingdom of Heaven was at hand everywhere they went.

What they were declaring was that the rules of the world's system now had to bow to a higher rule. The new king was Jesus, and His rules were above all other rules — including those of the Roman Empire.

When Moses went to the Pharaoh and said to him, "Let my people go!" he was also declaring that the Kingdom of his God was greater than Egypt.

When Daniel was told that a new rule in Babylon forbad anyone from praying to another God, and that anyone caught disobeying the rule would be executed, he continued praying three times a day as if that rule did not apply to him. He prayed, in fact, with his window open so that everyone could hear him.

When Daniel was taken to the lions' den, he still had his authority intact. He showed that he would never bow down to other gods, and that he believed his God would deliver him. This moved even the king. This authority was a result of Daniel having received wisdom from Heaven.

In the lions' den, the glory of the Lord was with Daniel, and the rules of Heaven applied. In the glory, in Heaven, and in the garden before the fall, animals did not kill humans. The act of animals turning on the crowning glory of God's creation was a result of the fall. Since the glory of Heaven filled the lions' den, the lions acted accordingly. They no longer remembered that they enjoyed eating human flesh. That was not normal in the glory and in the Kingdom of Heaven.

Jesus taught us to pray, *"Thy kingdom come, Thy will be done on Earth as it is in Heaven."* When Heaven's glory comes to the Earth, you can declare that the Kingdom of Heaven is at hand. And when you do, even the forces of nature must bow.

When David confronted Goliath, he was still very young. But he already had a revelation of his position seated in heavenly places. He had spent hours worshiping the Lord as the glory came down while he tended his father's sheep. When he heard the intimidating report concerning Goliath, it did not faze him. He went to Goliath with his heavenly authority and declared the victory that he had already seen in the glory. He did not look at his own size, age or experience. He knew that he had a covenant and a promise from God and that the giant did not.

God backed David up. Because Saul, a much larger man, did not have a revelation of his position in the glory, he was often insecure and frightened. David was never afraid.

Some years ago, we were trying to extend my wife's stay in France, and the official serving us was giving us a hard time. She insisted that my wife's birth certificate had to be officially translated into French before they could issue her any new papers.

Since we needed the papers that day, we didn't have time to have that translation work done. The woman went away for a few minutes, and I began to pray. I commanded that the authority of the French government bow the knee to the Kingdom of Heaven and treat us as ambassadors.

In a little while, the woman came back, and when she did, she asked me if I wanted two copies or three of the needed document. It almost seemed that she had completely forgotten the problem, and she gave us exactly what we needed.

The Kingdom of Heaven, the glory, is at hand, and God's promise will be quickly fulfilled: *"The earth will be filled with the knowledge of the glory of the Lord as the waters cover the sea."*

This is not to be confused with the popular teaching held by some that we will set ourselves up a kingdom and stay put right here, nor is it an excuse to disobey the laws of the land on a whim. This revelation takes us far beyond those carnal concepts and empowers us for greatness to glorify God in this present world.

Supernatural Wisdom Brings Favor Before Great Men

Wisdom and favor go together when it comes to speaking with world leaders, and both come from having the knowledge and revelation of the glory.

Joseph walked in such wisdom and favor that it brought him eventually into the presence of the king:

> *"And the patriarchs, becoming envious, sold Joseph into Egypt. But God was with him and delivered him out of all his troubles, and gave him favor and wisdom in the presence of Pharaoh, king of Egypt; and he made him governor over Egypt and all his house."*   Acts 7:9-10

When the Kingdom of Heaven is understood and declared or preached, the atmosphere changes. The revelation that the Kingdom of Heaven is here brings in that greater glory. When you declare what God is declaring, it begins to manifest wherever you are. Any place can be invaded with the glory of the Kingdom of Heaven, and every authority must bow to that Kingdom.

Philip went into a region where Simon the sorcerer was influential. People respected the man. When Philip came into town, however, the tables were turned:

> *And they heeded him [Simon] because he had astonished them with his sorceries for a long time. But when they believed Philip as he preached the things concerning the KINGDOM of God and the name of Jesus Christ, both men*

> *and women were baptized. Then Simon him-*
> *self also believed; and when he was baptized he*
> *continued with Philip, and he was amazed, see-*
> *ing the miracles and signs which were done.*
> Acts 8:11-13

As God is bringing new signs and wonders upon the Church, He is also giving us the favor and revelation to speak to any and all who are in authority so that we can reach many more people for God's glory. Alberto Motessi, an Argentine evangelist, preaches in crusades all over South America. There he fills stadiums with hundreds of thousands of people. He has often been called the Evangelist to the Presidents, for he has spoken with and led more presidents to the Lord than any other minister in South America. This is due to two elements: the simple favor and wisdom of God upon his life, and the great compassion he has for lost souls — whether they be presidents or bums on the street.

Ruth Ward Heflin walks in this same wisdom, glory and favor to speak to leaders. She has spoken to many world leaders, including the President of the United States, and recently to officials at the Pentagon. Doors have opened for her in many different countries to speak and prophesy to presidents and other high-ranking officials due to her revelation of her authority in the heavenly places. She knows that when God tells her to speak to the head of some government, the door will open — though she may not know a single person in that particular government.

The apostle Paul had the same revelation. Even in chains he spoke to the governor, Felix, and convicted him of sin. Felix admitted that he had been deeply influenced by Paul.

Paul eventually appealed to Caesar and was determined to speak to the leaders of the great empire in Rome. He ended his days in Rome, having spoken to many leaders and having influenced the entire known world for Christ.

John the Baptist had the same authority when he spoke, as did many other mighty men and women of God, both in the Bible and in the annals of history.

The preaching of the Kingdom of Heaven is one of the greatest last-day revelations and one the Church has yet to fully understand and apply. The wisdom and knowledge of God is being revealed to us so that we can walk in the fullness of what has been reserved for us all along.

Jesus told us to use the wisdom in the glory when speaking to rulers:

> *"Therefore be wise as serpents and harmless as doves."*   Matthew 10:16

God is still extending His favor to the Church. Whether your country is favorable to Christianity or indifferent, or if people are being thrown in prison and persecution has begun, the same glory applies. There have been seasons in which the Church has prospered and grown in favor with God and man, and there have been times of great persecution. Supernatural wisdom to speak to kings is not limited to ideal situations. The rulers of the world are subject to the glory of God when it manifests on the Earth through you — whatever the situation. God is looking for those He can use to speak to kings, for they wait to hear the word of the Lord.

Jesus promised us that this opportunity would arise.

> *"You will be brought before governors and kings for My sake, as a testimony to them and to the Gentiles."* Matthew 10:18

What do you say when God gives you an audience with a president, a banker, a judge, a police officer, a general, an actor, a warlock? You will only speak and do what you see your Father in Heaven saying and doing. Whatever comes from the throne will be backed by the authority and power of Heaven.

Jesus said:

> *"But when they deliver you up, do not worry about how or what you should speak. For it will be given to you in that hour what you should speak; for it is not you who speak, but the Spirit of your Father who speaks in you."*
>
> Matthew 10:19

Adam and Eve had authority over every living thing — as long as the glory of God was in the garden. They lost this in the fall. Now that God's glory is being restored, so is our authority and our favor with men. I believe that God will give you personal revelation and favor to speak to those in authority whom He has put on your heart.

Some of you will speak to presidents and heads of nations and bring them a timely word from the Lord. Some will be used as Esther, to change the heart of the king in favor of the Lord's people. And some of you will be used to open entire countries to the Gospel.

Many souls will be saved as a result of these efforts. Ask God for supernatural wisdom, and then do exactly as He tells you. His Word declares:

> *If any of you lacks wisdom, let him ask of God, who gives to all liberally and without reproach,*

> *and it will be given to him. But let him ask in*
> *faith, with no doubting, for he who doubts is*
> *like a wave of the sea driven and tossed by the*
> *wind.* James 1:5-6

Make that promise yours today, and you will find
your authority increasing proportionally.

Angelic Visitations

Then he dreamed, and behold, a ladder was set up on the earth, and its top reached to heaven; and there the angels of God were ascending and descending on it.

Genesis 28:12

Another of the miraculous aspects of this new move of God's glory is that we are beginning to see much more angelic activity. God is opening the heavens to His people. He is taking us into the heavens, and He is bringing the heavens down to us. Just as it has been said that the enemy, knowing that his time is short, is unleashing multitudes of demons upon the Earth, so God is releasing more angels to help us in this end-time harvest.

More and more believers are telling of being taken to Heaven and back. Others are seeing angels in their churches and in their homes. Some are seeing the Lord Jesus Himself. The gap between Heaven and Earth is being bridged. Jesus taught us to pray, *"Thy will be done on Earth as it is in Heaven,"* and this is becoming possible in the glory.

During the 1999 Summer Campmeeting in Ashland, Virginia, as more than a hundred teeth were changed into gold, I saw an angel being released into the camp to help in the revival. I began to declare what I was seeing in the Spirit.

Later, just as I was beginning to preach, we all heard singing. It was so strong and compelling that I had to stop speaking and listen. We all looked around, but no one was playing any of the musical instruments present, and no one was holding a microphone. The people stood to their feet in total silence as we listened to this heavenly singing.

All of us were surprised by this experience, while some were actually a little startled. It was awesome, to say the least.

After a few minutes, the music waned, and I was

released to continue speaking. From that moment on, there was such a powerful spiritual charge in the atmosphere that I knew something had changed. God had sent angels into our midst.

The Bible speaks of the ministry of angels:

> *Are they not all ministering spirits sent forth to minister for those who will inherit salvation?*
> Hebrews 1:14

Angels are used by God in many aspects of ministry — in healing, in signs and wonders, in protection, in communication, and in other ways as well. Angels are God's servants, and they carry out the orders of the King.

When the golden glory comes down, I always feel the presence of angels in our midst, and I know that Heaven is not very far away. All distance becomes relative in the glory.

My friend Billie Watts, the station manager of the TBN affiliate in Phoenix, Arizona, has had many experiences in this area, and often, as we have been preparing to do an interview, she has shared these experiences with me. She was also in one of the campmeetings in Ashland, where she shared an extraordinary experience.

Every evening Billie takes time to sit down at her piano and sing to the Lord. As she was worshiping

Him one evening, an angel came in through her patio door and stood before her. This was no ordinary angel. Of the many angels she has seen, this one, she said, was particularly large. "Huge" was the word she used. The angel was also the first one she had seen that was solid gold.

When the angel came near to the chair where Billie was sitting, he opened his hands, and she saw golden particles falling from his fingers. After he had left, she turned on the lights to make sure what she had seen had been real. There was gold dust all over the floor, on her legs, and on the chair.

I have come to believe that every time the gold manifestations begin to appear, angels are present to precipitate it. This is why we feel the atmosphere change. The same thing happens when other signs and wonders are seen. Angels are present.

It should not surprise us that angels are being seen more and more these days, for they played a significant role in the early history of the Church. When Peter was imprisoned, and the church prayed around the clock for his release, an angel came into the prison and let him go.

When Peter arrived at the place where the believers were praying and knocked on the door, a young maiden came to answer. When she told the others that Peter was at the door, they thought she had seen an angel. This again proves that angels were a normal part of the life of the early Church. It was not surprising to them that an angel could come and knock on their door.

Every time men or women of God have had an encounter with an angel, the experience has changed their lives. When an angel appeared to Mary, for instance, and declared that she would have a child, she was never the same again. Jacob wrestled with the Angel of the Lord, and he was never again the same. Moses' life also was completely changed after his encounter at the burning bush:

> *And the Angel of the LORD appeared to him in a flame of fire from the midst of a bush. So he looked, and behold, the bush was burning with fire, but the bush was not consumed.*
>
> Exodus 3:2-4

Just as in Bible days, angelic visitations today are serious experiences that often mark the opening of a new chapter in our lives and ministries. Angels deliver crucial messages from the Lord today, as they did in the case of Daniel. They bring with them not only direction, but also blessings and prosperity, miracles, warnings, impartations and gifts from Heaven to minister to us.

God sends angels to help us in times of transition. Even Jesus needed the ministry of angels during His earthly ministry:

> *And He was there in the wilderness forty days,*
> *tempted by Satan, and was with the wild beasts;*
> *AND THE ANGELS MINISTERED TO*
> *HIM.*   Mark 1:13

In every major revival, God has used angels. In Pensacola, I am convinced that a giant angel representing the holiness of the Lord facilitates the many who repent and are saved. This same thing is happening in Ashland and in Toronto, as well as in Argentina.

God releases new angels to churches and ministries when He is sending them a new anointing, revival or level of ministry. These angels bring with them the new glory to be revealed. It is always the Lord's power ministering to us, but it comes through the aid of angels.

In the great healing revivals, with men such as A.A. Allen and William Branham, angels were at work behind the scenes. These men often saw them and recognized them publicly. Even in Jesus' days, angels ministered God's healing power:

> *In these lay a great multitude of sick people,*
> *blind, lame, paralyzed, waiting for the moving*
> *of the water. For an angel went down at a cer-*
> *tain time into the pool and stirred up the water;*
> *then whoever stepped in first, after the stirring*

> *of the water, was made well of whatever dis-*
> *ease he had.* John 5:3-4

God is using angels in this present move of God to show signs and wonders, to enable us to bring in the harvest.

While I was in that jungle area of French Guiana and the gold dust appeared in many colors, the heavens were also opened to us. After the meeting, the pastor and I went to the room where we were staying, and there we began to talk about what had happened in the meeting. For some reason that I can't remember, the conversation switched to the subject of angels. Suddenly the atmosphere in the room changed. We ceased our conversation and began to worship God with all our hearts. That night, the heavens were opened to us, and until 4:30 the next morning we experienced angelic visitations.

Another pastor was staying in the same house. When he came into the room to say goodnight, he immediately dropped to the floor because of the awesomeness of the presence of heavenly beings.

We saw angels ascending and descending a ladder from Heaven, and as we began to describe to each other what we were seeing, we realized that our visions were identical. At certain moments, the glory would seem to wane for a few minutes, and we both would declare at the same time, "They are ascending again." We immediately thought of Jacob's experience.

Every time the angels would descend, both of us would feel an incredible surge of glory. These angels had just come from Heaven, and they were still carrying the glory of Heaven around with them.

When the angels would descend, they would also bring things from Heaven. We both were given some very special words from Heaven through those angels, and we both received new anointings. It was a life-changing experience for both of us.

At one point during the night, I saw a huge angel hovering over the pastor. I told him what I was seeing. He looked at me in amazement and asked how long I had seen the angel. I told him he had been there for about thirty minutes. He said his back had been feeling very hot for the past thirty minutes. God told the pastor that He had sent the angels to protect him from the attacks he would encounter as his apostolic ministry in Guiana was growing.

At that point, we moved into the kitchen, and it was even thicker with angels than the bedroom was. We began to worship the Lord again. I once heard Ruth Ward Heflin say, "We create the atmosphere for angels to manifest through praising and worshiping God," and I know she is right. When we got back to the bedroom, the angelic host had increased there as well.

Since the time of this experience, the pastor who was with me that night has had several similar angelic experiences that have changed his ministry even more.

The next day we took a small plane to Cayenne, the capital, where the mother church is located. As I was preaching in that church, I felt led to mention what we had experienced the night before. Many times experiences such as these are considered so sacred that we keep them to ourselves and don't tell anyone for years. That night, however, God told me to share the experience. He showed me that time is short and that He wants more and more people to be touched in this way.

When we share an experience and declare what we have seen, that realm is opened up to those who hear, and faith is imparted to them to step into it. That's exactly what happened the night I preached in Cayenne.

As I began to share my testimony, that same heavenly presence filled the church. When it came time for the altar call, I opened the altars to all those who would like to come forward and ask God to open the heavens over their own lives. I was about to pray for each of them, when the Lord spoke to me and told me not to touch anyone. His ministering angels would be my ministry team that night.

I walked among the people, and as I did, some

began to go into trances and have visions. Others were slain. Others began to weep and shake. Angels were ministering as I walked among the people. It was very exciting. It dawned on me that I would always have a ministry team to help me wherever I happened to be.

During that final service, many souls were saved. This included several who were delivered from witchcraft. At the end of the service, I declared that these heavenly visitations would continue for some through the night. What they later told me was very exciting, and I will get to it in the next chapter.

7

Transported in the Spirit

*Now when they came up out
of the water, the Spirit of the
Lord caught Philip away.*
Acts 8:39

I made my declaration in Cayenne,
French Guiana, that heavenly visitations would continue throughout the
night, and the very next day we began to get reports of people being
taken to Heaven. The pastor's
daughter was one of them. After the
meeting, she had gone to a friend's
house to spend the night. There, in

the room where she and the friend slept, she was caught up into Heaven in the Spirit. The mother of the house came into the room while this was happening and saw the pastor's daughter in a sort of trance. The girl was talking, but she could not understand at the time what she was saying. Concerned, she tried to shake the girl out of this trance state, but she could not. What concerned her was that she heard the girl say, "Please, don't send me back. I'm so happy here." Still, she was powerless to intervene.

Transported to Heaven and Back

When the pastor's daughter finally came to herself, she explained what had happened. She had been taken in the Spirit to Heaven. There she saw the city, she saw a river, and she saw Jesus. After she had visited with Jesus for a while, He told her it was time to go back to Earth. She still had things to do down here for His Kingdom. That was when she had been overheard begging to stay.

While in Heaven, she saw her friend, and she told the friend that she had seen her there. The friend replied that she had also been taken to Heaven and had seen the pastor's daughter there as well.

To test her friend, the pastor's daughter asked what they had talked about in Heaven. When her friend told her, it was the same conversation she remembered the two of them having in Heaven. I am sure that the two of them were taken to Heaven together in the Spirit in this way so that they could encourage each other in their mutual experience in the future.

When I was in Heidelberg with Pastor Pierre Fey, I mentioned during the meeting that God was allowing His people to see Heaven. God did many wonderful things for us during those meetings: the people's hands began to drip with supernatural oil, and we had several teeth filled with gold. The next week, Pastor Fey called me to say that his daughter was taken to Heaven for twenty minutes.

Being transported to Heaven is nothing new. Paul had this experience:

> *I know a man in Christ who fourteen years ago — whether in the body I do not know, or whether out of the body I do not know, God knows — such a one was caught up to the third heaven. And I know such a man — whether in the body or out of the body I do not know, God knows — how he was caught up into Paradise and heard inexpressible words, which it is not lawful for a man to utter.*
>
> 2 Corinthians 12:2-4

Although this is not a new experience, it is new to

many in our time, but Heaven wants to be discovered more than we want to discover it.

We have managed to explore the far reaches of the Earth, the depths of the sea, and even planets that are billions of miles away. Man has also set foot on the moon. So Heaven is the next and final frontier.

Just as astronauts are able to bring back samples from other planets, we can bring back something from Heaven. The gold and diamonds appearing in our meetings are only the beginning of this phenomenon.

Transported From Place to Place Here on the Earth

As we have seen, in the glory there is no time as we know it. What takes us years to accomplish on the Earth is done *"in the twinkling of an eye"* in Heaven's glory. That glory manifested upon the Earth will produce the same effect as it would in Heaven. Because the glory is an accelerator, God will accelerate everything upon the Earth through the glory, including travel from place to place.

In the past, many believers have experienced being transported by the Spirit of God to some other place. Some have been transported in both body and spirit, while others have been transported only in spirit. This is an experience that God is now restoring to the Church.

One biblical example that always comes to mind is that of Philip. Although there are several other passages of scripture that deal with this subject, this is the best-known one:

> *Now when they came up out of the water, the Spirit of the Lord caught Philip away, so that the eunuch saw him no more; and he went on his way rejoicing. But Philip was found at Azotus. And passing through, he preached in all the cities till he came to Caesarea.*
>
> Acts 8:39-40

Recently this experience has been reported as happening in China. There, a certain evangelist has reportedly been transported to many of the main cities to preach the Gospel. It is a vast nation with a vast population, so evidently God is helping His servants to reap the harvest there more quickly.

It happened to Renny McLean when he was invited to preach in Kenya. He was waiting for confirmation from the Lord as to whether or not he should go, when one night he had a dream. He was speaking in Swahili in his dream, and he saw that great miracles, healings and salvations were taking place. He took this as a confirmation that he should go, and six weeks later, he was in Kenya preaching.

When he arrived at a small village, the people said

they were very happy to see him again, but they wondered why he had returned so soon. When he told them that he had never been to Kenya or even to Africa, they showed him people who had been touched and healed when he last came. He asked them when it had happened, and they said six weeks before. He had been transported to Kenya in the Spirit while he slept and was used of God there without even realizing that it was more than a dream.

John G. Lake, the great healing missionary to South Africa, had a similar encounter, which is documented in his writings. He was alone in his room one night, interceding for the healing of a woman who lived in another area. The next day he saw the woman, and she thanked him for coming to her house in the middle of the night to pray for her. She had been totally healed. He explained to the woman that this was impossible. He had been at home, although he was praying for her. The woman said she had seen him come into the room, pray for her, and then leave. All she knew was that she was healed.

Recently, during a meeting in Louisiana, I had a very unusual experience. The Lord gave me the first and last name of a man. I asked if a man by that name was in the building, and no one responded. Then, a woman raised her hand and said that I was calling out her husband, but he was at home. Without knowing anything about the man, I called out in the Spirit three times, commanding him, "Come back!"

The next day, the woman came forward to testify. Her husband had been in a coma for four days. The moment I called out his name during the meeting, he came out of the coma, and he was now up and eating, something he had not been able to do in a very long time. She was very excited about his miracle.

There is no distance in the glory. We can pray over someone in the Spirit, and it will be as if we were there physically praying for that person. Our human spirits, when they are yielded to the Holy Spirit, can reach a person when we cannot physically be there.

There is a dimension in which we can be in two realms at the same time. A similar thing happens to us when we are daydreaming. We can be sitting in a classroom physically, but our minds and thoughts are elsewhere. In this same way, we can be in one place physically, and our spirits can be somewhere else entirely.

This often happens during times of deep intercession. While we are interceding for a certain country, God may take us there.

There is no limitation in the glory. We are made up of a body, a mind and a spirit, and our spirits are mobile.

This happened to Jesus too:

> *Then the devil took Him up into the holy city,*
> *set Him on the pinnacle of the temple and said*
> *to Him, "If you are the Son of God, throw Your-*
> *self down. For it is written:*
> *'He shall give His angels charge over you.' "*
>
> Matthew 4:5-6

How could Jesus have been in the desert one minute and then on top of a pinnacle in Jerusalem the next? He had to be transported there. This was not a vision, for Jesus could not have been tempted if He had not really been there.

These things also occurred in Old Testament times. When Elijah was taken to Heaven in a whirlwind, the other prophets looked for him, thinking that he had been transported to some other place:

> *Then they said to him, "Look now, there are*
> *fifty strong men with your servants. Please let*
> *them go and search for your master, lest per-*
> *haps the Spirit of the* LORD *has taken him up*
> *and cast him upon some mountain or into some*
> *valley."*
> *And he said, "You shall not send anyone."*
>
> 2 Kings 2:16

Apparently, this was a common happening with Elijah, and these younger men had seen it before. This time, they could not find the prophet. He had received a one-way ticket to Heaven, as had Enoch before him.

The prophets, however, continued to believe that Elijah had been transported, and insisted on searching for him:

> *But when they urged him till he was ashamed, he said, "Send them!" Therefore they sent fifty men, and they searched for three days but did not find him.* 2 Kings 2:17

They searched for Elijah for three days (a three-day journey was a long way to be transported in those days), but they *"did not find him."*

Ezekiel was transported in the Spirit in a similar manner:

> *The hand of the Lord came upon me and brought me out in the Spirit of the Lord, and set me down in the midst of the valley; and it was full of bones.* Ezekiel 37:1

In the days ahead, as we become more and more acquainted with this realm of glory, we will come to realize just how unlimited it is. Distance is nothing in the glory, and God can easily transport us from place to place.

The apostle Paul carried many concerns for the

young churches throughout the Roman Empire, but because he traveled so much, it was sometimes impossible for him to be physically present to deal with some of their problems. This did not seem to limit him. He wrote:

> *For though I am absent in the flesh, yet I am with you in spirit, rejoicing to see your good order and the steadfastness of your faith in Christ.*   Colossians 2:5

How is it possible that Paul was *"absent in the flesh"* (meaning that his body was not there) and still he rejoiced *"to see [their] good order and the steadfastness of [their] faith in Christ"*? I believe that Paul meant this literally and that he was taken in the Spirit to them.

Sometimes Paul had to deal with serious problems of sin in the churches, problems that threatened to destroy the church. When he could not be there in the flesh, he walked into another realm, one in which there was no distance. Having been taken to the various churches in the Spirit, he was able to deal with the person or the situation. For instance, Paul wrote to the Corinthian believers:

> *For I indeed, as absent in body but present in spirit, have already judged (as though I were*

> *present) him who has so done this deed. In the*
> *name of our Lord Jesus Christ, when you are*
> *gathered together, along with my spirit, with*
> *the power of our Lord Jesus Christ, deliver such*
> *a one to Satan for the destruction of the flesh,*
> *that his spirit may be saved in the day of the*
> *Lord Jesus.*   1 Corinthians 5:3-5

Paul even claimed that when the Corinthians were gathered together, he would be there in the meeting in the Spirit and would know everything that was happening. How could this be? The Spirit often gives us prophetic dreams in which we are alerted to some plan that has been hatched against us or our ministries. I am convinced that these are more than dreams, that we are actually being taken to a place to observe a situation, so that we can know what is happening and act accordingly.

The Counterfeit

Such experiences, of course, are not unique to Christian believers. Many of those who are involved in the New Age movement have had what they call "out-of-body experiences." The same is true of people involved in witchcraft and other demonic activities. This is logical because the enemy is a counterfeiter. He can only copy and pervert. He cannot create, for there is only one Creator.

Lucifer knew how things operated in Heaven's glory. He knew not only the glory, but also the knowledge of the glory, how things worked in the spirit realm. It should not be a surprise to anyone that he has released this knowledge (in a perverted sense) to the world.

We should be moving in realms of the glory beyond anything that Satan can copy or pervert. If witches are able to tap into the supernatural realm for evil purposes, how much more should we be able to discover in the supernatural how to have access to the depths of the mysteries of God's glory! He will surely release to us access to realms that no unsaved person can ever enter.

Many of the people who are involved in the occult have a great hunger for the supernatural, and they have not found much in the church that can match what they have seen in the enemy's camp. It is time to accelerate in the glory realm, and many of those who are in darkness will be saved as a result.

A Further Step: Transported in Time

We know that a person can be taken to Heaven and back, and we know that a person can also be transported from one place to another on Earth. There is, however, another dimension to this revelation — traveling or being transported in time.

There is no time or distance in the glory. Past, present and future are all relative in Heaven. God knows the end from the beginning (see Jeremiah 1:5). He knew us before we were created in our mothers' wombs, and He has known our destiny from the beginning.

Several years ago there was an interesting and funny movie that came out called *Back to the Future*. It was so successful that it spawned sequels. This is a subject that has intrigued men for centuries. Many novels have been written about traveling to either the future or the past. Such time travel, however, is not as "imaginary" as one might think.

Many years ago, during an altar call with many other young people at a summer camp, I was taken in the Spirit to Hell. I saw the flames and felt their heat. I saw people screaming out in pain and agony. Their flesh was being burned, and they were utterly destitute and hopeless. It was the most awful thing I have ever seen.

Then I saw my father in Hell, and I broke down and wept for him. In actuality, my father was still living (and is today), but I was being shown the future.

I saw my father burning and crying out like the others. Then he turned to me and, with tears in his eyes, said, "Why did you stop praying for me? I was so close to being saved."

I repented that day for having given up on my father's salvation, and I wept as I had never wept before. I could not accept the fact that my father would be in Hell, and I cried out to God for my father to be saved.

Then I heard the voice of God telling me to continue interceding (I was the only person still praying for my father at the time). As I interceded for him, the Holy Spirit prayed through me.

Suddenly I sensed a release and a great peace. When I returned home from the summer camp, I discovered that my father had accepted the Lord. I asked him when it had happened, and he told me the story.

On the very day and hour that I had seen my father in Hell, he had been poised with a gun to his head, ready to end his life. Because of my intercession, God sent an elderly lady by to visit him. She saw what was happening and led my father to the Lord. That experience birthed an evangelistic call upon my life. I had been taken into the future and was able to see something before it happened. The experience also changed my father's destiny.

I believe that many of the Old Testament prophets were transported to see the future and bring back some revelation concerning it to the people of their time. Isaiah wrote:

Surely He has borne our griefs
And carried out sorrows;
Yet we esteemed Him stricken,
Smitten by God, and afflicted.
But He was wounded for our transgressions,
He was bruised for our iniquities;
The chastisement for our peace was upon Him,
And by His stripes we are healed.

Isaiah 53:4-5

How could Isaiah claim that Jesus had already borne our sorrows, that He was bruised and wounded (all in the past tense), when Jesus had not even been born yet in human flesh? Isaiah was surely taken to a place and time in the future, and there he saw the cross. When he returned to his time, he wrote about what he had seen, as if it had already been done. After all, he had seen it happen.

Much of the Old Testament looks forward to the cross, and all the healings and miracles and resurrections performed there were because of the power of that future event. They were possible only because Jesus would pay the price for salvation, for healing, and for deliverance. Isaiah had foreseen it, as did many others.

When we need something from God, we usually base our faith on a past event or a past scriptural promise. The prophets of the Old Testament based their faith on a future event, and they were still able to see the same results.

When the people were saved under the Old Testament through animal sacrifice, it was but a shadow of that which was to come. For the shadow to exist, an object must exist that creates the shadow. An invisible or nonexistent object cannot create a shadow.

The object is much more real than the shadow. The events of the cross were so real that they cast a shadow over all of history. The fact that it was a future event meant nothing to eternity.

Abraham saw something in the future, and this caused him to offer up his son Isaac, to sacrifice him, just as Jesus would be sacrificed. He even believed that Isaac could be raised from the dead (since he was still a child of destiny). How could Abraham have had faith to carry out his mission (exactly as Jesus would) and to believe that Isaac would be raised from the dead (when the resurrection from the dead was not yet known)? I believe he caught a glimpse of the future in the Spirit and brought that truth back to the people of his day.

Sometimes we have dreams, and they come to pass. Other dreams don't seem to be fulfilled, but is it perhaps because we see some evil that will befall us or our loved ones or our friends, and we intercede before the Lord and prevent it from happening? Sometimes we wake up to find ourselves calling upon the Lord, binding the enemy or speaking in tongues. God is showing us the future and using us to prevent its occurrence. Then we come back to the present.

When that future event catches up with us, we may see circumstances identical to those we experienced in our dream. We will discover, however, that the battle has already been won.

Another case of time travel occurs when the Lord shows us the future He has prepared for our lives or our ministries. It is then up to us to reach out and lay claim to it. Again, Paul wrote:

> *For we are His workmanship, created in Christ Jesus for good works, WHICH GOD PREPARED BEFOREHAND THAT WE SHOULD WALK IN THEM.*
>
> Ephesians 2:10

As we have seen, there are future events — frames — that are prepared for us to walk into. There are promises that have been spoken over our lives. The moment those promises were spoken, they were already created. They may be future, but they are just as real as anything we can touch today. As we walk into these promises, they will be actualized. The Bible speaks of tasting *"the powers of the age to come"*:

> *... and have tasted the good word of God and
> the powers of the age to come.*   Hebrews 6:5

This is not nearly as difficult as we might think,
and it certainly is not impossible. The glory that is
awaiting us (future tense) in the age to come in
Heaven can be brought into the present upon the
Earth. We can walk into a dimension of the heavenly realm that has been prepared for our future.

Bringing Future Promises Into the Present

The Promised Land was already created and waiting for the Israelites. They only had to walk into it,
and it would be theirs. Many of them failed to realize, however, that the future was already created.
They were waiting for God to do something about
the giants that lived in the land. The truth is that
these "giants" were terrified of the children of Israel, having heard the stories of the Exodus from
Egypt and of the many miracles related to their trek
through the wilderness. All the Israelites had to do
was obey God and walk into the land, and the battle
would have been easily won. Instead, they waited
another forty years, remaining in the past, and most
of that generation never made it into the land.

When Jesus told Peter to catch fish, even though
he had tried all night and caught nothing, the fish

were already there waiting to be caught. They were there from the moment Jesus had spoken them into existence. Peter had simply to walk into what had already been prepared.

Last year Ruth Heflin prophesied over us that television ministry would begin to open to us. Once she spoke it, the event was already created (but in a future tense), ready to be walked into. I had to step into that future promise. I obeyed the leading of the Holy Spirit and called someone I knew who works with television. Within a short time, those doors began to open.

When Jesus rose from the dead, other dead people rose from their graves and walked around the city of Jerusalem. That was a foretaste of what will happen when *"the dead in Christ will rise"* (1 Thessalonians 4:16). The people of Jerusalem were tasting *"the powers of the age to come"* because Jesus had walked into the future event prepared for Him.

How can we say that the cross was a future event that Jesus simply needed to walk into? Again, Revelation speaks of *"the Lamb slain from the foundation of the world"* (Revelation 13:8). He was slain from the beginning of creation. The future was already prepared for Jesus, long before man fell in the garden. When Jesus came to the Earth, it was to walk into what had already been prepared for Him.

With God, time is different. Past, present and future are not the same in His eyes as in ours. He sees them all at once and has control over them all. Time is His servant.

Delaying and Reversing Time

I believe God can use His people to delay and even reverse time. When Jonah went to Ninevah to reveal to the Ninevites that God was about to destroy them, they quickly repented. This reversed the time clock of judgment, and judgment was prevented — although God had told Jonah that it would surely come.

God was about to destroy the Israelites in the wilderness, but Moses saw the future and interceded for them. His faith was based on their destiny, not just their past, and through his prayers, time was reversed.

There have been many prophecies given over certain cities (such as Los Angeles) that they would be destroyed because of sin. Many of the people in the churches where these prophecies were given began to fast and pray and repent for the city, and the judgement was delayed or even averted.

Years ago, when I was working with a certain church, God began to direct us into itinerant evangelism. The problem was that we were also needed in the church we were serving. My wife and I both had dreams of preaching in new places, to new faces, and we saw that miracles, signs and wonders would follow our ministry and that a great harvest would be reaped. A new and fresh anointing came upon us, and we began to receive other invitations for ministry. It was clearly time for us to move on.

As I contemplated telling the pastor what we were feeling, I had a dream in which the pastor showed me a new office he had prepared for me. He was offering me a whole new phase of ministry and asking me to make a commitment to stay for a much longer period of time.

In the dream, I told the pastor that I appreciated the offer, but that I could not accept it because God had been directing us to other fields. When I said this, the smile left his face, and it was suddenly filled with rage. He commanded us to stay, but I stood firm on my commitment to the new vision God was giving us.

When I woke up, I felt as if the dream had somehow really happened. I could not explain it at the time, but it seemed that I had actually gone to the future and dealt with the situation. Normally, it would have been very difficult for me to "let someone down" like that, but the Lord was teaching me about obedience — even when it brings misunderstanding. He was showing me that I must not allow the fear of man to dominate any area of my life.

When I next saw the pastor, he called me into his office and offered me a new position, exactly as I had dreamed. I thanked him and explained to him what God had been directing us to do. He looked disappointed at first, but minutes later he was admitting that he, too, had sensed a new anointing upon our lives and had an idea that we were being led in a different direction.

We stayed on for a few more months, so that there could be a smooth transition of leadership, and we left that church with the blessing of the pastor. I believe that I was able to take care of a future event in my dream, letting the enemy know that I would not compromise what God was showing us. When the actual future event occurred, the fit of rage I had seen in my dream did not manifest itself. There was a more blessed reaction. Creating a scene like the one I saw in my dream and leaving the church on bad terms could have damaged our future ministry. God took us to the future and let us deal with it, and I am thankful.

God can take you to a future event in the Spirit during prayer, while you are sleeping, or even in broad daylight. When it happens, you have faith to bring that future event and turn it into a present event by declaring, prophesying, obeying and praying it into existence — against all odds.

France has always been known as a difficult country for the Gospel. Many have said that it could not be revived. When God gave me a vision concerning France and other parts of Western Europe, I was translated to a future event. I saw revival breaking out across Paris and the rest of France and throughout Europe.

In 1998, the Lord told me to declare prophetically that revival would begin in Paris, and as I have told earlier, three weeks after the meetings began, He told me to declare that France would win the World Cup soccer tournament against Brazil. This would be a sign of the favor of God over France for revival. This also seemed impossible, and even the French had no faith that their team could win.

When France won the World Cup that year, the pastor of the church decided that we would continue the meetings. That first wave of revival went on for the next six months.

We can affect time and history. We can slow time down to avert disaster, or we can accelerate time for the sake of the harvest. It happens when we allow God to transport us to the future. This is what the Scriptures mean when they say:

Where there is no vision, the people perish.
Proverbs 29:18, KJV

When it looked as if President Clinton was about

to be found guilty at his impeachment trial, God told Ruth Heflin to stand in the gap and declare that this effort would not prosper. She had seen what God intended for the future of the country. The Lord showed her that the conviction and removal from office of the President would have adverse effects on the economy of the country. She kept praying and declaring that the President would finish his term.

The night before the final decision was to be made (and it seemed certain that the President would indeed be convicted), she stood in front of the White House and prayed for him one last time. The Lord prayed through her with tears for the presidency. The next day, the trial ended with a verdict of not guilty. Time had been reversed for America's President.

If America had judged Mr. Clinton for his sin, then God would have had to send judgement upon America. Those casting the stones were not free of sin themselves. The President had recognized his moral failure and had repented on national and international television, the first American President to do so.

This is not to say that we accept everything the man does. The important thing is that we pray and do as God instructs, even if we don't quite understand God's mercy or judgement. We may never quite realize how history was reversed, both in the United States and around the world, as a result of one woman's obedience.

God used Joshua to reverse time for Israel. A battle was being waged, and the forces of Israel were faring well. They would need another twenty-four hours, however, to win the battle. Joshua acted by faith and commanded the sun to stand still in the heavens. It worked. The battle was won.

In a video shown at the Brownsville School of Ministry, David Hogan, a missionary to the Native Americans in Mexico, relates a similar story. A little girl had fallen down on some rocks and smashed her head. It was so severe that her brains were splattered on the rocks. When the people saw this, the Lord instructed them to just worship Him, and as they worshiped, the glory came down. When they had worshiped the Lord for more than four hours, the little girl came back to life, and her head had not even a scratch. God had recreated her brain and put everything back into its place. Still, the brains she had lost were there on the rocks as proof of the miracle that He had done.

Time had been reversed, as if that child had never fallen on the rocks. We have seen many healings and miracles that left not a trace of the sickness. Scars instantly disappear in the glory of God.

Just as time is running out, the glory is coming in.

Eternity will soon replace time. As we enter into deeper realms of glory, time will seem less and less of an obstacle to the purposes of God in this generation. Let God transport you to new realms in His Spirit today.

Miraculous Unity

So I prophesied as I was commanded; and as I prophesied, there was a noise ... and the bones came together, bone to bone. Ezekiel 37:7

Through the revival of God's glory, He is bringing a unity to the Body of Christ that can only be described as miraculous. Just as the glory draws souls to the light, it also brings together those believers who seek the same glory and the same harvest. Many groups that have been separated throughout the years (because of some doctrinal difference or emphasis) are finding themselves unified in meetings where the glory is manifested. This unity is important to continued revival.

Many groups of Christians have been seeking revival. The problem is that they are like the bones in the valley of Ezekiel's vision. They are completely separated from one another. Before God can bring life and resurrection to the dry bones, He must bring them together to form the essential elements of the Body.

The bones of the valley of Ezekiel's vision came together when Ezekiel prophesied, and as we declare and prophesy into existence this new move of God, something is happening behind the scenes that is very wonderful.

A lot of the shaking that has come with this new move of God's Spirit is the result of His bringing the bones together. As the popular song says, *"There's a whole lot of shaking going on."*

In the process of coming together, the bones are shaking off the dryness of the past and the pettiness that has separated believers. Then, as we see bone joined to bone, the Church is beginning to look more and more like the real Body God intended it to be.

Before God can place the breath of life in us and cause us to experience revival and resurrection power, there has to be something substantial for Him to raise up. He does not want to resurrect just a foot, an arm, or a shoulder. Many of us are like those separated bones. We want resurrection, but what would we be if God did resurrect us? It would be strange if a hand was resurrected without the rest of the body attached to it. God could resurrect it, but even if He did, such a hand would be limited.

Flesh on the Bones

The coming together of the bones in Ezekiel's vision was just a first step. Once the bones were together, God continued to work on them:

> *Indeed, as I looked, the sinews and the flesh came upon them, and the skin covered them over; but there was no breath in them.*
>
> Ezekiel 37:8

God formed the bodies of Adam and Eve first, then He breathed life and resurrection power into their nostrils, and that is the correct order of things. Sometimes churches want to see a major harvest of souls, yet they can hardly unite a few churches behind an evangelistic crusade. The Body needs some major work done on it before it is ready to be raised up. We need God to put some flesh on our bones.

The next wave of revival that we see will be of

supernatural unity. It will come as God speaks and brings bones together and puts flesh on them. He can do it, when we cannot. The bones are first shaken into place, and then God begins to form the flesh upon them.

This same process was performed on the early Church. Before God brought the disciples together in the Upper Room, they had been scattered. Jesus' arrest and crucifixion threw their little group into confusion and chaos. When they came together again, God breathed resurrection life into the Church, and it came to life again.

In his own case, Ezekiel, as we have seen, had more prophesying to do:

> *Also He said to me, "Prophesy to the breath, prophesy, son of man, and say to the breath, 'Thus says the Lord GOD: "Come from the four winds, O breath, and breathe on these slain, that they may live." ' "*   Ezekiel 37:9

God is sending His glory upon the dry bones to bring them together, He will put flesh upon them, and then He will breathe life into them corporately.

The Breath of God

Many groups have seen the need for more unity,

and have been working on this problem. They now need a second wave, the wind of resurrection power, to complete the work. Many already have the form — the body, the flesh on the bones — and everything is looking great. The only problem is that there is no life in the body. When this is the case, we must speak to the breath to revive the dry bones. This is what Ezekiel did:

> *So I prophesied as He commanded me, and breath came into them, and they lived, and stood upon their feet, an exceedingly great army.*
> Ezekiel 37:10

God wants to raise up a great army, and one of the most important elements in any army is unity.

Carlos Annacondia, perhaps the most effective evangelist of our time (having led more than two million souls into a relationship with Jesus), says that the key to his ministry is unity. He has been known to cancel an upcoming crusade if it comes to his attention that there is no unity among the "cooperating" pastors. If he sees that pastors and churches are in competition and cannot work easily together, he feels that his efforts could be better spent elsewhere.

He has canceled crusades at times, even after advertising has been done, a tent was in place, and intercessors had been praying for the upcoming meetings. This is a bold step, but he does it because he knows that there can be no lasting harvest without unity. The first wave of unity must be in place for the breath of life to come into a city.

As we have seen, the disciples knew what it was to fish and have no results:

> *[Jesus] saw two boats standing by the lake; but the fishermen had gone from them and were washing their nets.*
>
> *When He had stopped speaking, He said to Simon, "Launch out into the deep and let down your nets for a catch."*
>
> *But Simon answered and said to Him, "Master, we have toiled all night and caught nothing; nevertheless at Your word I will let down the net."*   Luke 5:2 and 4-5

Once unity is in place, Jesus can give the command, and the harvest will come in.

The Enormity of the Catch

Many have toiled long and hard to get just a few fish for their ministry or church, and they now dream of a great harvest. But what would we do if such a harvest came? Are our nets strong enough to hold that many fish? Would our nets not break under the weight of responsibility? God wants to give us souls, but we have to be able to handle those souls once they come to us.

First, we must do what is necessary to strengthen our nets, and then they will have the endurance to handle the millions of souls that will come into them.

Catching fish is only the beginning of the work. Afterward they must be cleaned and prepared. It is a great task. When God's great harvest begins, there will be no time for competition or jealousy. Each of us will have his hands full, as there will be much to do for the Master. Now is the time to get ready.

Once the preparations are made, the catch is guaranteed:

> *And when they had done this, they caught a great number of fish, and their net was breaking. So they signaled to their partners in the other boat to come and help them. And they came and filled both the boats, so that they began to sink.*   Luke 5:6-7

We must be mending and strengthening our nets and calling other boats to help us in the great harvest to come, for it will take all the help we can get. Even though Peter called in another boat, the nets were breaking, and both boats began to sink. Even

with the help of others, he and his companions
barely had the strength to bring in the miraculous
catch.

We cannot do this work alone. We need many
more boats, many other churches and ministries, to
come alongside and to reap with us. We need men
and women with strong nets of love and unity in
the glory.

The Lord of the Harvest in Control

As always, the first requirement for harvest is that
we allow Jesus, the Lord of the Harvest, to sit in the
boat and that we give Him control of the situation.
This is what Peter did.

The moment Jesus sat down in Peter's boat and
began to give directions, everything began to prosper. We must let the glory take over our lives so that
we can clearly hear the Lord's instructions.

If we are willing, the Lord of the Harvest will cause
unity to come forth. It is not our ambition, but His
glory, that others must see in us. Some of us might
be good organizers, but it is the glory of God that
will bring the right bones together.

Jesus prayed:

> *"That they all may be one, as You, Father, are
> in Me, and I in You; that they also may be one*

in Us, that the world may believe that You sent Me. And the glory which You gave Me I have given them, that they may be one just as We are one: I in them, and You in Me; that they may be made perfect in one, and that the world may know that You have sent Me, and have loved them as You have loved Me."

John 17:21-23

Jesus knew that it was the glory that would make us one. The glory brings a supernatural unity that is impossible to attain with our own human efforts. In the glory of Heaven, there are no divisions, and that is what our Father wants to see among His children here on Earth.

A Prophetic Vision

A few years ago, I had a prophetic vision concerning unity in the Body of Christ. It came to me during an extended time of prayer for revival and harvest. The vision was so real to me that I was not sure if I was sleeping or awake, whether I was dreaming or seeing a vision.

I watched as the army of God arose. It was like a modernized replay of World War II. I saw vast armies being mobilized all over the world. What the

Lord revealed to me through this vision was very clear.

First, He took me to the Book of Ezekiel and showed me the four living creatures that appeared to the prophet:

> *As for the likeness of their faces, each had the face of a man; each of the four had the face of a lion on the right side, each of the four had the face of an ox on the left side, and each of the four had the face of an eagle.*
>
> *And each one went straight forward; they went wherever the spirit wanted to go, and they did not turn when they went.*
>
> Ezekiel 1:10 and 12

The Eagle:

In my vision, the eagle represented our modern satellites, able to detect targets so that bombers could hit them with precision. Eagles fly so high that they see things from a much different perspective. They can spot enemy targets well in advance. This is the prophetic gifting that God is establishing among us to meet our need for intelligence in this war. Just as technology has advanced in this regard, so will the gifts and equipping of the Holy Spirit for the last-day harvest. If we learn to use our new equipment, a maximum number of souls can be saved with a minimum number of casualties.

The Ox:

The ox is a work animal. I saw that once the eagle had done its work of spotting the targets, the ox served as an airplane to release bombs, tanks and artillery. These aircraft were able to fly low enough to destroy strategic targets on the ground, removing all obstacles and making clear paths on which ground troops could advance.

The ox is the symbol of a new breed of intercessors. These will not simply destroy everything in their paths, but will work with the prophetic, so as not to waste their valuable time. They will only hit designated targets. Prophetic intercession will be successfully accomplished by the eagle and the ox working together.

The Lion:

Next, I saw the lion. The lion represents the great evangelistic thrust that has come (and is coming) on the entire Body of Christ. These are the ground troops. Once the targets are spotted and the strongholds dismantled and destroyed, the lion can take over, capturing enemies and setting prisoners free. The lion then can declare that the battle has been won and enforce the victory with a roar.

If the first two creatures had not done their jobs, the victory in no way could have been won. But even if they have done their jobs well, the harvest still must be taken.

At the end of World War II, even though Germany had lost and victory had been declared, that victory had to be enforced. Many people continued to die — even after the war had been officially declared over. The battlefield was vast, and enemy soldiers had to be notified that their side had lost the war, and they had to be captured and disarmed.

The lions in my vision had authority to speak to the enemy, and he had to obey them.

I saw that the ground troops had medical staff able to heal the wounded on the spot and even raise the dead. The great evangelistic thrust will be accompanied by great demonstrations of healing, miracles, deliverances and resurrections.

Once the lion had taken over the city and fortified it, bound the enemy and delivered the prisoners, these prisoners were placed on trucks and sent to hospitals.

The Man:

The last of the four creatures had the face of a man. I saw that the man represented the shepherd and pastoral giftings. Once the new prisoners had arrived at the hospital ward, these shepherds would first heal and restore them. The rescued men would be fed and attended to and given any required surgery. In the process, they would receive a totally new life.

Once the prisoners had recovered, they would move to another section of the hospital, where they would be trained for battle. When they were ready, they would be sent out to some of the same places they were once held prisoner. They would know the enemy well, and would thus be a great asset to the war effort.

In the coming harvest, many hundreds of thousands of people will move into the pastoral gifting — without necessarily having to be the key person in their churches. Many will simply be gifted in healing, feeding and training and building up new converts.

Following the Spirit:

Again, of these four creatures, Ezekiel said:

> *And each one went straight forward; they went wherever the spirit wanted to go, and they did not turn when they went.* Ezekiel 1:12

This is the strategy we must follow. Whatever direction the Spirit shows us to go, that is always the key to victory. Sometimes it will be the time and season for the prophetic to lead the way, while at other times it will be the intercessors who will lead. Some-

times it will be time for the evangelistic gift to have
its voice heard, and at other times, the Spirit will
lead the pastoral giftings or some of the other gifts
in the Body to become the principal voice at the moment. The Body will begin to operate as a body, all
the disparate parts working in unison.

The creatures of Ezekiel's vision did not turn as
they went. When there was a new obstacle in the
way or when a new direction was needed for some
other reason, they stopped and let others lead, as
the Holy Spirit directed. If we would learn to let the
Holy Spirit lead, we could save so much wasted time
and avoid going in the wrong direction, with the
wrong people, at the wrong time. This is important
because timing is now more critical than ever before.

We must simply follow orders from our General
and Friend, trusting His prosecution of the war effort. No war could be won if everyone did as he
wished. Imagine what would happen if ground
troops decided on their own when and where they
would go and what they would do, disregarding the
commands of their superiors. Soldiers who did this
might find themselves fighting the wrong troops.

Imagine what would happen if bombers did not
wait for instructions and began to destroy the wrong
targets, only to learn later that they had killed their
own men or their allies. It is time to take our proper
places so that we can win the war that is before us,

and this requires the miracle of supernatural unity in the Church. There is no other way that can we function as one.

This clearly is the Lord's will:

And He Himself gave some to be apostles, some prophets, some evangelists, and some pastors and teachers, for the equipping of the saints for the work of ministry, for the edifying of the body of Christ, till we all come to the unity of the faith and of the knowledge of the Son of God, to a perfect man, to the measure of the stature of the fullness of Christ. Ephesians 4:11-13

The Parts of the Engine Work Together:

When I was seeing this vision, I also saw the engine of a car. The Lord showed me that for the Body of Christ to walk in full power and glory, all the parts must be in place and working together.

Sometimes an engine will run even if some of the spark plugs are not in place or if there is a leak in the water or oil. Although it may run, however, it won't run well, and it will eventually break down. If some elements of the engine are not well connected, the engine cannot even start, let alone run.

This is also true of the Body of Christ. God is bringing the pieces together, for each of us has something to contribute, something so vital to the welfare of the whole that its absence can often make the difference between victory and defeat. As Paul wrote:

> *... from whom the whole body, joined and knit together by what every joint supplies, according to the effective working by which every part does its share, causing growth of the body for the edifying of itself in love.*   Ephesians 4:16

When every part is doing its share, the fullness of God's glory will come into place, and this will cause a major growth in the harvest. Are you joined and knit together with your brothers and sisters in God's glory? Are you aware that *"every joint supplies"* something to the Body? The more we are joined to the glory of God, the more we will find our places and function together. Apart from the glory, our activities can be little more than man-made programs and *ideas* of unity. Unity is a miracle that only the Spirit can do for us.

A Return to Our Roots

Then He said to me, "Son of man, these bones are the whole house of Israel."
Ezekiel 37:11

There is yet another element to this unity, one that will unleash the fullness of the supernatural power of God when it is finally in place.

There is much being talked about concerning unity and reconciliation among the various denominations, movements and races in the Church. At the same time it is happening in the Church, the world is also attempting to unite diverse elements that live alongside each other in various regions of the world. It seems that the world has also caught onto a renewed revelation that unity brings power.

We know that even greater things are prepared for us than for the early Church, since the latter will be greater than the former. Still, most believers have yet to taste the fullness of the power the believers of the early Church walked in on a day-to-day basis. This included the raising of the dead and citywide outbreaks of revival on a continual basis. This will come, for God has promised to bring us the former and the latter rain together.

As we venture into the new, however, we cannot forget where we came from. We must rediscover our roots and their power, and we would do well to examine closely what caused the power of the early Church to dwindle. This is important if we are to possess the fullness of what has been reserved for this generation.

While I was on a recent ministry trip to Israel, God began to release to me some very crucial revelation in this regard. He did some great signs and wonders and miracles there, and we openly shared with the Jewish people concerning their Jewish Messiah. We were able to do this in congregations, but also in hotels, in hospitals and even with rabbis praying at the Wailing Wall, and the results were very exciting.

Israel has had the reputation of being a hard country for the Gospel, but this is suddenly changing. The new wave of glory affecting the Church has splashed over onto the Jewish people, and wonderful things are happening all over Israel.

God began to show me while I was in that blessed land some important things concerning this next move of His Spirit. He is about to unleash His resurrection power as we have never seen it, yet this power must be tapped into or pressed into, and this requires a concerted effort. Certain things must be contended for, as the greater glory requires a greater yearning and desire. Any price we pay will be well worth the victory we will receive.

"The Whole House of Israel"

As we have seen, Ezekiel prophesied to the dry bones, and they began to come together. Once they were in place, flesh was formed on them. Then God sent His breath upon them and brought them back to life. Ezekiel, however, tells us something else very important in that same chapter. Again, he said:

> *So I prophesied as He commanded me, and breath came into them, and they lived, and stood upon their feet, an exceedingly great army.*

*Then He said to me, "SON OF MAN, THESE
BONES ARE THE WHOLE HOUSE OF IS-
RAEL. They indeed say, 'Our bones are dry,
our hope is lost, and we ourselves are cut off!' "*
Ezekiel 37:10-11

These were not just any dry bones. They were *"the
whole house of Israel."* The Jewish people have, indeed, been dry for the past two thousand years, but
God is raising them up and giving them new life.
This resurrection to new life for the Jewish people
will release fresh resurrection power over the entire
Body of Christ.

With Ezekiel, it took one prophecy to bring the
bones together, and it took a second prophecy to
breathe resurrection life into them. What would the
third prophecy do?

*Therefore prophesy and say to them, "Thus says
the Lord God: 'Behold, O My people, I will open
your graves and cause you to come up from
your graves, and bring you into the land of Israel. Then you shall know that I am the Lord,
when I have opened your graves, O My people,
and brought you up from your graves. I will
put My Spirit in you, and you shall live, and I
will place you in your own land. Then you shall
know that I, the Lord, have spoken it and performed it,' says the Lord."* Ezekiel 37:12-14

"I will place you in your own land." Surely the return of the Jewish people to their homeland is an indication of the season in which we find ourselves. This was part of God's promise to the people of Israel. They would be placed in their own land, and something more: they would be resurrected from spiritual death. God promised to place His Spirit within His people after He had restored them to their land. Just as we have seen the first part of the promise fulfilled, we will also see the entire fulfillment of this promise — and soon.

Reconnecting to the Roots

Now what does this have to do with us? The Church was born when Jewish men and women loved the Messiah, followed Him and preached His Word to the ends of the Earth. The restoration of the Jewish people to their Messiah will bring even greater power to the world in these last days, and we will again be connected to our roots.

A flower can usually only last two days without being connected to its roots, yet the Church has been disconnected from its Jewish roots for two thousand years now. We are entering the third day of our disconnect, and God is bringing about unity and rooting us back into the source of power and blessing that originally graced the Church.

As we have seen, unity brings power, and God is bringing about the greatest union of all — Jew and Gentile. God did not design the Church to be two — a Jewish Church and a Gentile Church. He has made of us both one Body.

Part of the purpose for God sending this current wave of glory upon the Church is so that we can draw the Jewish people to their Messiah. As we do this, we will be tapping directly into the blessing, favor and resurrection power of God reserved for His chosen ones.

Paul had a similar revelation:

> *For if their being cast away is the reconciling of the world, what will their acceptance be but life from the dead?*   Romans 11:15

If the fall of the Jewish people brought about blessing to the Gentiles, how much greater blessing will come to those who work to restore God's people back to Him through their Messiah? And how much greater blessing will come to those who work toward the reconciliation and union of God's chosen people with the rest of us who believe?

The early Church began as all-Jewish, but was eventually composed of both Jew and Gentile. We Gentiles came into the Church because Jewish believers caught a burden and revelation for the whole world. Their willingness to reach out to all men everywhere allowed for the power and glory of God to be released in its fullness, and this same coming together of Jew and Gentile will bring about another wave of the fullness of God's glory upon the Body of Christ. It is time to get plugged back into our spiritual roots.

The Church is but the wild branch that was grafted in, yet we have enjoyed the benefits and become partakers of the fatness of the olive tree:

> *For if the firstfruit is holy, the lump is also holy; and if the root is holy, so are the branches. And if some of the branches were broken off, and you, being a wild olive tree, were grafted in among them, and with them became a partaker of the root and fatness of the olive tree, do not boast against the branches. But if you do boast, remember that you do not support the root, but the root supports you.* Romans 11:16-18

Because Jesus, a Jew Himself, brought salvation to a small group of devoted Jewish men and women, salvation was made possible for all men. Our roots are in Israel, the Jewish people and the Jewish Messiah. Christianity is a branch of this root system that was formed much more than two thousand years ago.

Blessing the Jewish People Blesses Us

Today, God is leading more and more of us to bless Israel by blessing the Jewish people. We can do it through fasting and prayer and intercession, and we can do it through supporting and uniting with Messianic Jews who are witnessing to their own people. In doing this, we lose nothing. That same blessing and power that we direct toward them comes back on us.

Jews do not always understand the Gospel as we do. They must be presented with a Jewish Messiah and a Jewish faith, not necessarily with our Western ways. Our effort must not be to make them like us, but to bring them to Messiah. It is we who must return to our roots, not the other way around.

Paul was blessed with a very effective ministry, and one of the keys to his effectiveness was blessing his Jewish people. He wrote:

> *I say then, have they stumbled that they should fall? Certainly not! But through their fall, to provoke them to jealousy, salvation has come to the Gentiles. Now if their fall is riches for the world, and their failure riches for the Gentiles, how much more their fullness!*
>
> Romans 11:11-12

Because of Israel's fall and rejection of the Messiah, salvation, riches and the glory of God have come to the Gentiles. That does not mean that Israel will always remain alienated from her Messiah. Israel's recovery will bring about an even greater release of salvation, power, favor and riches upon the Body of Christ.

Paul magnified and multiplied his ministry by making the Jews jealous and bringing them to salvation:

> *For I speak to you Gentiles; inasmuch as I am an apostle to the Gentiles, I magnify my ministry, if by any means I may provoke to jealousy those who are my flesh and save some of them.*
> Romans 11:13-14

The glory of God upon the Church is the only thing that will provoke the Jewish people to jealousy today. They have known His glory better than anyone else has known it, and they will respond to its manifestation.

When the Jewish people have seen the miracles God is doing today — miracles of gold fillings and gold crowns, and the miracle of the gold dust — this has stirred them to jealousy. Signs, wonders and miracles (which are manifestations of the glory) have proven to be an effective tool in reaching the Jewish people. This is surely because it is a manifestation of the glory they once knew and for which they continually long.

The Source of Our Separation

Sadly, the Church (for the most part) has often tried to remove or, at best, hide the Jewishness of the Gospel. It is no wonder that for many years Jews have not been able to relate to a Gospel that portrays Jesus as a Gentile Savior, when the Scriptures clearly promised that He would be Jewish.

The early Church, made up of both Jewish and Gentile believers, was powerful and shook the world with the Gospel. When did this power begin to wane? Interestingly enough, it seems to have happened about the time the Roman Empire stopped persecuting Christians. Until that time, believers were being burned at the stake and fed to the lions.

Oddly enough, during the years of severe persecution, Christians remained united. Their revolution was turning the world upside down, and even Roman soldiers were impressed by the faith of these men and women whom they were commanded to torture and murder. Many soldiers were saved as a result of this. It is said that some Roman soldiers insisted on joining the Christian believers in being put to death because of what they had witnessed.

As the Church became more and more Gentile, something happened that I believe is responsible, more than anything else, for cutting off the power the early believers once knew. A hatred and distrust of the Jewish people arose, and eventually an outright persecution of them.

The Fateful Decision at Nicaea

The following statement was dictated at the Council of Nicaea in A.D.325 and was sent out to all the churches:

> *From the letter of the Emperor [Constantine] to all those not present at the council (Eusebius, Vita Cons., Lib, III, 18-20):*
> *When the question relative to the sacred festivals of Easter arose, it was universally thought that it would be convenient that all should keep the feast on one day; for what could be more desirable than to see this festival, through which we receive the hope of immortality, celebrated by all with one accord and in the same manner? It was declared to be particularly unworthy for this, the holiest of festivals, to follow the customs of the Jews, who had soiled their hands with the most fearful of crimes, and whose minds were blinded. In rejecting their custom,*

we may transmit to our descendants the legitimate mode of celebrating Easter; which we have observed from the time of the Savior's passion (according to the day of the week).

WE OUGHT NOT THEREFORE TO HAVE ANYTHING IN COMMON WITH THE JEW, FOR THE SAVIOR HAS SHOWN US ANOTHER WAY; OUR WORSHIP FOLLOWING A MORE LEGITIMATE AND MORE CONVENIENT COURSE (THE ORDER OF THE DAYS OF THE WEEK): AND CONSEQUENTLY IN UNANIMOUSLY ADOPTING THIS MODE, WE DESIRE, BRETHREN, TO SEPARATE OURSELVES FROM THE DETESTABLE COMPANY OF THE JEW. For it is truly shameful for us to hear them boast that without their direction we could not keep the feast. How can they be in the right, they who, after the death of the Savior, have no longer been led by reason but by wild violence, as their delusion may urge them? They do not possess the truth in this Easter question, for in their blindness and repugnance to all improvement they frequently celebrate two Passovers in the same year. We could not imitate those who are openly in error. How then can we follow these Jews who are most certainly blinded by error?

For to celebrate a Passover twice in one year is totally inadmissible. BUT EVEN IF THIS WERE NOT SO, IT WOULD STILL BE YOUR DUTY NOT TO TARNISH YOUR SOUL BY COMMUNICATION WITH SUCH WICKED PEOPLE [THE JEWS]. YOU SHOULD CON-SIDER NOT ONLY THAT THE NUMBER OF CHURCHES IN THESE PROVINCES MAKE A MAJORITY, BUT ALSO THAT IT IS RIGHT TO DEMAND THAT OUR REASON AP-PROVES, AND THAT WE SHOULD HAVE NOTHING IN COMMON WITH THE JEWS.

(*The Nicaean and Post-Nicaean Fathers,* Vol. XIV, Willam B. Eerdmans Publishing Company, 1979, pgs. 54-55)

Apparently, because Constantine was able to stop persecution against Christians, the Gentile believers accepted this new concept of separation from the Jewish roots of their faith. Tired of being thrown to the lions, they relaxed in Constantine's era of peace. The problem was that, by accepting this heresy, they compromised their power, unity and faith. They had, in essence, agreed to a divorce, and separated themselves from their Jewish brethren. This compromise cost the lives of many more people throughout the ages than would have been true if the persecution had continued. The unity of the early Church was destroyed, and Gentile believers were cut off from their roots. This could only spell tragedy.

As a result of the Council of Nicaea, persecution against Jews became almost commonplace. During the second and third centuries, the "Church Fathers" unleashed a cruel discrimination campaign against the Jews and against anything Jewish — including much of what we have come to call the Old Testament. Author Marvin Wilson writes in his book *Our Father Abraham* (William B. Eerdmans Publishing Company, 1991): "Furthermore the Church Fathers taught that the unfaithfulness of the Jewish people resulted in a collective guilt which made them subject to the permanent curse of God."

This separation from the Church Fathers eventually resulted in a spirit of anti-Semitism, and this was the cause of such mass killings as the Inquisition and the Holocaust, all done in the name of Christ and the cross. In my opinion, it was this divorce from the Jews and our Jewish/biblical roots that brought about the Dark Ages. Noted Christian author Rick Joyner has also mentioned in his writings that most divisions in the Body of Christ can be traced to the division between the Church and the Jewish people.

Martin Luther's Attitude Toward the Jews

Martin Luther came onto the scene in the sixteenth century to restore the Church from the Dark Ages back to the original message of salvation by grace through faith. At first, Luther recognized the importance of the Jewish people and declared that they were not cut off. Unlike his predecessors, he saw the need to restore the Jewish people to salvation, and he attempted to evangelize them.

The problem was that by then the Jews had endured so much persecution and slaughter in the name of the Church that they were not willing to listen to Luther. Their rejection of him left him with deep wounds, and he also turned against the Jews.

Luther became so bitter against the Jewish people that he began a series of writings and articles against them entitled *"The Jews and Their Lies."* In these writings, Luther labeled the Jews as "venomous thieves" and "disgusting vermin." Seeds of hatred and anti-Semitism were once again being transmitted throughout the Church.

During the years 1542-1543, Luther produced several writings, all of which showed a bitter animosity against Judaism and the Jewish people. He said such things as:

> *A man who doesn't know the devil may well wonder why the Jews, above all others, are so hostile towards Christians. Moreover, they are so without cause, for we show them all goodness. They live here among us and have the use of our land, streets, and lanes while our leaders*

*are sitting back, snoring open-mouthed, allow-
ing them to lift from their purses and coffers,
and to steal and rob them as they fancy. How?
By allowing their subjects and themselves to
be fleeced and impoverished by the usury of the
Jews, and so, with their own money, they make
themselves beggars.*

Luther suggested that Jewish houses should be de-
molished, that the right of Jews to safe conduct be
taken away, and that there be a prohibition against
usury. He went further in suggesting that able-bod-
ied Jews, both men and women, be used for slave
labor, and that all their synagogues and schools
should be burned. Fortunately, evangelical leaders
of the day did not follow Luther's proposals.

Today, leading Lutheran theologians have openly
and clearly dissociated themselves from their
founder's anti-Jewish views. We thank God for using him to rediscover the truth concerning salvation,
yet we lament his shortsightedness in rejecting the
Jewish people and our Jewish roots.

Other organized churches have been shown to be
anti-Semitic. The Roman Catholic Church, in recent
years, has made amends for its shortcomings in this
regard. In a prayer by Pope John XXIII, intended for
use in the Catholic Church worldwide, one can read
the following words:

> *Today we are aware that many, many hundreds of years of blindness have veiled our eyes, causing us to lose sight of the loveliness of Your chosen people, and to fail to recognize in their faces the characteristics of our favoured brethren. We are aware that the mark of Cain brands our foreheads. Throughout the centuries, our brother Abel has been shedding tears, lying in the blood which we spilled. We are the cause of this by forgetting Your love. Forgive us for the curse we have wrongly linked with the Jewish name. Forgive us for having crucified You afresh in their bodies. We were ignorant of what we were doing.*

Recently, Pope John Paul II visited Israel. He went to the Wailing Wall, where he placed a letter between the cracks of the large stones asking forgiveness for the blindness and sin of the Catholic Church toward the Jewish people in the past. He also visited Yad Vashem, the Holocaust Museum, and talked with Holocaust survivors. Whether or not these acts were done with pure motives is not for us to judge. The result of his historic visit is that Jewish people everywhere have become more tolerant of Christian believers and more open to the possibility of Yeshua being their Messiah. This can only help speed up what God is trying to accomplish.

Despite the fact that many Christians claim no association with the Pope, the Jewish people see him as the leader of the Christian Church as a whole. Any such move in the direction of reconciliation and repentance can only bring about more openness to the Gospel.

Whether or not we identify with any of the larger traditional churches, as believers, we are nonetheless personally implicated in the inheritance of our fathers — both good and bad. We cannot afford to repeat the mistakes of the past concerning the right relationship of the Church to the Jewish people, but some present-day theological teachings assert otherwise.

Modern Anti-Semitism

Replacement theology has been the most destructive and effective theology in separating the Church from the Messianic movement and the understanding of Israel in the last days. This is the teaching that promotes the belief that the Church is "spiritual Israel" and has replaced Israel as God's chosen people. Replacement theology takes solely for the Church all the promises that were made to the Jewish people.

At first glance, some biblical passages might seem to indicate what some anti-Semites are teaching:

> *For he is not a Jew who is one outwardly, nor is circumcision that which is outward in the flesh; but he is a Jew who is one inwardly; and circumcision is that of the heart, in the Spirit, not in the letter; whose praise is not from men but from God.* Romans 2:28-29

Most Messianic Jews agree that Gentile believers do make up "spiritual Israel," in the sense that they have been grafted into the promises of Israel. But, the extreme teaching of replacement theology, that the Church has replaced Israel, is refuted by many other passages, including all of Romans 9-11 and verses like the following from the same book:

> *What advantage then has the Jew, or what is the profit of circumcision? Much in every way! Chiefly because to them were committed the oracles of God.* Romans 3:1-2

Paul the apostle foresaw the problem that would arise after his passing and addressed it in this, his letter to the Roman believers:

> *And if some of the branches were broken off, and you, being a wild olive tree, were grafted in among them, and with them became a partaker of the root and fatness of the olive tree, do*

not boast against the branches. But if you do boast, remember that you do not support the root, but the root supports you.

You will say then, "Branches were broken off that I might be grafted in." Well said. Because of unbelief they were broken off, and you stand by faith. Do not be haughty, but fear. For if God did not spare the natural branches, He may not spare you either. Therefore consider the goodness and severity of God: on those who fell, severity; but toward you, goodness, if you continue in His goodness. Otherwise you also will be cut off.   Romans 11:17-22

The fact that we were grafted in does not mean that we replaced the entire tree.

The Call to Unity

In this present move of God, a call is going forth to again form one Body of Christ. This Body is to be made up of both Jewish and Gentile believers. Will we heed the call and reconnect to our spiritual roots? If we are willing to do so, we will experience, in the days just ahead, a new surge of the power of God and will see the greatest harvest ever recorded.

Already Jews are being drawn to the Messiah in record numbers. Destiny is knocking at the door. We must heed the call to support the preaching of the Gospel *"to the Jew first."* God has promised that in the last days there would be revival in modern-day Israel:

> *And they also, if they do not continue in unbelief, will be grafted in, for God is able to graft them in again. For if you were cut out of the olive tree which is wild by nature, and were grafted contrary to nature into a cultivated olive tree, how much more will these, who are natural branches, be grafted into their own olive tree?* Romans 11:23-24

God does not want us to be *"ignorant of this mystery"*:

> *For I do not desire, brethren, that you should be ignorant of this mystery, lest you should be wise in your own opinion, that blindness in part has happened to Israel until the fullness of the Gentiles has come in. And so all Israel will be saved, as it is written:*
> *"The Deliverer will come out of Zion,*
> *And He will turn away ungodliness from Jacob;*
> *For this is My covenant with them,*
> *When I take away their sins.*
> Romans 11:25-27

A mystery is something that can only be understood by revelation (as every other truth, including salvation). Just as we needed a revelation of Jesus in order to be saved, so we need a revelation of Israel and the Church to understand the importance of our union with every believer for the last-day harvest. In the days to come, this will be a key issue for the Church.

God has never been unfaithful to fulfill a covenant with His people. He is a covenant-making God. We can be sure that His promises will be fulfilled, and we are nearing the time of their fulfillment.

The fulfillment of God's full promise to the Jewish people will prepare the way for His return. To get ready for that day, He is lifting the veil from our eyes, so that we can see clearly to help our Jewish brethren find their way home. Jesus said to the Jews of His day:

> *"See! Your house is left to you desolate; for I say to you, you shall see Me no more till you say, 'Blessed is He who comes in the name of the LORD!' "*   Matthew 23:38-39

The time of the fullness of the Gentiles is nearing its end, and we have a dual commission from the Lord. All nations must hear His Word before the end, and *"all Israel [must] be saved"* before the end.

"One New Man"

God is forming *"one new man"*:

> *For He Himself is our peace, who has made both one, and has broken down the middle wall of separation, having abolished in His flesh the enmity, that is, the law of commandments contained in ordinances, so as to create in Himself one new man from the two, thus making peace, and that He might reconcile them both to God in one body through the cross, thereby putting to death the enmity.* Ephesians 2:14-16

God is bringing together two bodies, one Jewish and one Gentile, and making them one. This does not mean that we will be identical. Each of us is unique, and each of us has something to contribute to the whole. The Messianic Jews have already received revelation and truth that will be beneficial to the Church, and the Church has much to offer the Jews. Our coming together will form a powerhouse for the Lord.

Many of the feasts of the Old Testament contain powerful symbolism that can unlock revelation and the power of God for us. They are prophetic and show us what is to come. This does not mean that non-Jewish believers need to look Jewish and celebrate everything exactly as Jewish believers do. It means that despite our differences we can come into a oneness and a mutual understanding of the graces, revelation and truths that have been given to each of us. We are like two different shoes, and both are needed to make the pair.

Jesus said that He had not come to destroy the Law and the prophets, but to fulfill them. The wonderful presence of God's glory that comes to us when we celebrate the Communion in the Spirit is also experienced by Jewish believers when they celebrate their feasts. Jesus celebrated those same feasts, and that included the Passover meal that we have come to call the Last Supper. Both the Church and the Jews have a rich common heritage.

The Time for Uniting Has Come

The Messianic movement is growing considerably, and very soon there will be a unity between the Gentile Church and the Messianic movement to form *"one new man,"* as the Lord has desired. We must do all within our power to bring it to pass swiftly.

Many Christians are having a hard time dealing with the Messianic movement, and often it is because they don't see it as part of the Body of Christ. To become part of the Body of Christ, they consider, these Jewish people will have to conform to "the church." Messianic believers have sometimes been mistrustful of the Gentile Church and have purposely kept themselves separate. This has not helped Gentile believers understand the Jews.

At the same time, we must say that if the Messianic movement had been assimilated into the Gentile Church, Jewish believers would have lost their Jewish identity. There is a reason for the miraculous preservation of the Jewish people and the Messianic movement.

The Messianic movement has been attacked from two sides. Orthodox Jews have not seen Messianic believers as Jews, and Gentile believers have not seen them as true Christians. God loves each of the branches, and will now merge them into *"one."*

There were prejudices at work in the time of the early Church, and the apostles were forced to deal with them. They made it clear that God made no distinction between Jewish and Gentile believers concerning salvation and the grace of God. Other distinctions, however, were agreed upon by the elders during a council held in Jerusalem (see Acts 15:6-29). For this reason, some apostles were sent to the Gentiles, while others were sent to the Jews.

It is important for us to understand why Jewish believers of the first century continued to observe the rituals of the Law, fully realizing that they were not saved by the Law. When Paul returned to Jerusa-

lem after an extensive trip among the Gentile nations, he had a discussion with the local leaders:

> *When he had greeted them, he told in detail
> those things which God had done among the
> Gentiles through his ministry. And when they
> heard it, they glorified the Lord. And they said
> to him, "You see, brother, how many myriads
> of Jews there are who have believed, and THEY
> ARE ALL ZEALOUS FOR THE LAW."*
>
> Acts 21:19-20

Paul, who was called *"the apostle to the Gentiles,"*
was the greatest defender of the grace of God and
freedom of the Spirit, yet he himself was about to
show that he also understood the need to observe
the rituals of his people:

> *"But they have been informed about you that
> you teach all the Jews who are among the Gen-
> tiles to forsake Moses, saying that they ought
> not to circumcise their children nor to walk ac-
> cording to the customs. What then? The
> assembly must certainly meet, for they will hear
> that you have come. Therefore do what we tell
> you: We have four men who have taken a vow.
> Take them and be purified with them, and pay
> their expenses so that they may shave their*

> *heads, and that all may know that those things
> of which they were informed concerning you
> are nothing, but that you yourself also walk
> orderly and keep the law. But concerning the
> Gentiles who believe, we have written and de-
> cided that they should observe no such thing,
> except that they should keep themselves from
> things offered to idols, from blood, from things
> strangled, and from sexual immorality."*
> *Then Paul took the men, and the next day, hav-
> ing been purified with them, entered the temple
> to announce the expiration of the days of puri-
> fication, at which time an offering should be
> made for each one of them.*   Acts 21:21-26

Was Paul doing this to attain salvation according
to the Law? Of course not! No one understood the
error of salvation through the Law better than he.
He was honoring the Lord's own commandments
to the Jewish people, his culture and his heritage.

James reassured the believers that, *"concerning
Gentiles,"* it was not necessary for them to observe
all the Jewish rites. There are certain things, however, that the Jewish people have been commanded
to observe throughout all generations. The first
apostles understood that these were not demanded
of the Gentiles, and they were not required to perform them, but Jews continued to do so.

Messianic believers must understand that the Gentiles are not second-class citizens in the Kingdom of God simply because they do not follow all the Jewish laws. For their part, Gentile believers must understand the Lord's command to the Jewish people, that they are to retain their uniqueness as a people, and that they are still to be included in the Body of Christ — the *"one new man."*

The covenant that God made with Abraham was twofold. We love the part that declared, *"In you all the families of the earth shall be blessed."* All believers can apply this promise to bless the Earth with the Gospel. The other part of Abraham's promise is just as valid, although it was primarily for the Jewish people. It foretold that Abraham's seed would be given land as an everlasting possession.

The alienation of Gentile believers from their Jewish roots was a tragedy. The rejection that Martin Luther felt from the Jews caused him to react badly and to say things that have led to teachings like replacement theology and even to a justification of the Holocaust. At the same time, many Messianic leaders have held to a replacement theology of their own, claiming that the Messianic movement will somehow replace the Church. This also is a reaction to the horrible persecution Jews have endured through the centuries.

It is time for forgiveness and reconciliation from

both parties. There is power in forgiveness. Let us all rise above all limiting theologies that have emerged from wounds and counterwounds. It is time to heal all wounds and to receive reattachment to our roots. Until we are all healed, until we forgive and are forgiven, we cannot see clearly each other's position. Let God's Spirit do the work of restoration and form the *"one new man"* of God's will.

Paul wrote to the Galatians:

> *For you are all sons of God through faith in Christ Jesus. For as many of you as were baptized into Christ have put on Christ. There is neither Jew nor Greek, there is neither slave nor free, there is neither male nor female; for you are all one in Christ Jesus. And if you are Christ's, then you are Abraham's seed, and heirs according to the promise.*
>
> Galatians 3:26-29

This could not mean that men and women are not different. Who could deny that there is serious distinction between males and females? Still, we unite to form couples and families. This proves that the Lord is not trying to bring about a unity of conformity between Jew and Gentile, but a unity in diversity. If the leaders of the early Church came to the conclusion that they could walk in unity in diversity (and they walked in greater power than most of us), reuniting with our roots will surely bear fruit for us as well.

A New Sign

Recently, a remarkable discovery has taken place in Israel to confirm these truths. A symbol was discovered on pottery used by the early Church. Among the artifacts recently discovered bearing this symbol is a brick-shaped piece of local marble inscribed with the Messianic seal and the words in Aramaic: "For the Oil of the Spirit."

This piece of marble seems to have been the base for a vial of anointing oil. A small pottery piece with the same Messianic seal was found nearby. These were found, along with some sixty others, in a grotto now called The Sacred Baptismal Grotto of James the Just and the Apostles on Mount Zion in Jerusalem. James the brother of Jesus was the leader of the first-century believers in Jerusalem. Their place of worship was believed to be on Mount Zion.

In 1990, Ludwig Schneider, editor-in-chief of the magazine *Israel Today* struck up a friendship with an old Greek Orthodox monk who lives as a hermit in the Old City of Jerusalem. One day the monk showed Schneider a cache of artifacts that he had secretly excavated on Mount Zion before the Six-Day War in 1967. Schneider was taken aback. Many of these pottery shards, oil lamps and stone pieces were engraved with an unknown symbol. The symbol consisted of a menorah at the top, a Star of David in the center, and a fish at the bottom.

Schneider was immediately convinced that this must have been a symbol of the first Jewish-Christian congregation.

The monk then led Schneider to a cavity in the rock adjacent to the Tomb of David and the Upper Room on Mount Zion and told him that this is where he found the artifacts. Today, the cave is dark and musty and sealed off with iron bars.

These would have been the earliest known artifacts from the Church, yet for ten years after their discovery, they have been kept secret. Ludwig

Schneider approached the Israel Museum with the artifacts and was promised that they would be put on display. So far, this has not happened. It seems that the authorities are hesitant to reveal the mystery of the Messianic seal to the people of Israel.

Today, we often use the fish symbol on bumper stickers on our cars. Many do this without even wondering where it originated. The fish symbol, however, is only half of the truth. The other half was cut out of Christian symbols, along with everything else Jewish, after the Council of Nicaea in A.D. 325. The menorah and the star of David belong with the fish to form the entire symbol.

The fish, in that sense, has become a symbol of our lack. We are running on only half the power, revelation and unity that the early Church knew. As we plug the pieces back together (much like a key is inserted to turn the ignition and start an engine), the power God intended us to have will come roaring back. As we allow God to combine the Jewish and Gentile believers into one Body, we will begin to walk in the fullness of what has been reserved for us.

God's Desire for Jerusalem

Before leaving Jerusalem on my last trip there, I began to seek the Lord concerning the city of Jerusalem itself. I asked the Lord what His plans were for the city in the near future. Many people have differing views concerning God's timetable for the city, so I wanted to hear from the Lord. The Lord began to speak to me of revival coming to the Holy City.

What a place to have revival! We often speak about revival returning to the United States, England and other countries that once experienced a move of God, but what better place for a revival than Israel? After all, the very first Christian revival took place there.

The Lord showed me that the same way people fly into cities that are currently spiritual centers of revival in various parts of the world, people from all nations (the saved and the unsaved alike) will come to Jerusalem in the days ahead, because of the glory of the Lord that is evident there.

What the Lord showed me is not to be confused with the New Jerusalem of which the Scriptures speak. He was speaking of the modern city of Jerusalem:

> *For thus says the L*ORD *of hosts:*
> *"Just as I was determined to punish you*
> *When your fathers provoked Me to wrath,"*
> *Says the L*ORD *of hosts,*
> *"And I would not relent,*
> *So again in these days*

I am determined to do good
To Jerusalem and to the house of Judah."
                                        Zechariah 8:14-15

God is once again ready to bless the ancient city of Jerusalem. In fact, He's already doing it. I have never sensed the presence of God's glory as I do when I am in Jerusalem. When we were in the Upper Room this last time, my wife and I led a young Korean man to the Lord. He, like many others, had come to Israel searching for God.

The first time we had gone into the Upper Room ourselves, we had had a very powerful encounter that changed our lives and ministry. I wrote of it in my first book, *Desperate for New Wine* (Renew, 1998).

This confirms God's promise:

> *"Thus says the LORD of hosts:*
> *'Peoples shall yet come,*
> *Inhabitants of many cities;*
> *The inhabitants of one city shall go to another,*
> *saying,*
> *"Let us continue to go and pray before the LORD,*
> *And seek the LORD of hosts.*
> *I myself will go also."*
> *Yes, many peoples and strong nations*
> *Shall come to seek the LORD of hosts in*
> *Jerusalem,*

And to pray before the LORD.'
Thus says the LORD of hosts: 'In those days ten
men from every language of the nations shall
grasp the sleeve of a Jewish man, saying, "Let
us go with you, for we have heard that God is
with you." ' "   Zechariah 8:20-23

We have yet to see this promise come to pass in
the city of Jerusalem, but it will happen. This is why
it is so important to pray for Israel and for the city
of Jerusalem in particular.

This does not mean that Jerusalem will always be
popular, but there is something unique about the
city that sets it apart from all others. After all, it is to
Jerusalem that the Lord Himself will one day return.

The Promise of Joel

When Peter quoted the prophet Joel on the Day
of Pentecost, he did not quote him completely. Peter quoted:

"But this is what was spoken by the prophet
Joel:
'And it shall come to pass in the last days, says
God,
That I will pour out of My Spirit on all flesh.

*And it shall come to pass that whoever calls
upon the name of the LORD shall be saved.'* "
                                    Acts 2:16-17 and 21

There was more to Joel's prophecy, but the reason Peter did not finish quoting Joel was because
some of what Joel had said was reserved for our
time. Joel declares:

*And it shall come to pass
That whoever calls on the name of the LORD
Shall be saved.*
*FOR IN MOUNT ZION AND IN JERUSA-
LEM THERE SHALL BE DELIVERANCE,
AS THE LORD HAS SAID,
AMONG THE REMNANT WHOM THE
LORD CALLS.*   Joel 2:32

Ruth Ward Heflin has often said that one sees the
rest of the nations through Jerusalem. Just as revival
has come to many parts of the world, it has come to
the Holy City. At present, there are some five hundred rabbis in Israel who are secretly born again.
This is known among quite a few believers in Israel.
It is said that when the number reaches a majority,
they will then reveal their faith to the entire nation.

Recently, I was led to go to the Wailing Wall after
a meeting at Christ Church. It was already past mid-

night, and the crowd was much thinner than usual. While I was praying at the Wall, the Lord led me to prophesy to one of the rabbis who was there too. I went to a chief rabbi and prophesied to him that God would visit him and personally reveal to him the Messiah so that he could lead many others to Him.

When I had finished speaking, the rabbi thanked me for speaking to him. A more normal reaction (in the past, at least) might have been for the rabbi to interrogate me or raise a great fuss and arouse the security guards. He did not, and through this God confirmed to me that something new is already happening in the city of Jerusalem. Now is the time to share our faith there — as the Spirit leads.

How can you be a part of this end-time harvest among God's chosen people? You can fast and pray for all Israel and for the Jewish people. You can sow into ministries that are reaching Israel and the Jewish people. And you can be a witness yourself.

James declared to the elders of the first-century Church:

> *"Men and brethren, listen to me: Simon has declared how God at the first visited the Gentiles to take out of them a people for His name. And with this the words of the prophets agree, just as it is written:*
> *After this I will return*

*And will rebuild the tabernacle of David, which
has fallen down;
I will rebuild its ruins,
And I will set it up;
So that the rest of mankind may seek the LORD.
Even all the Gentiles who are called by My
name,
Says the LORD who does all these things.' "*

Acts 15:13-17

Jerusalem, Center of Activity

I truly believe that the last great revival will come out of Jerusalem. It was the spiritual center of revival in the beginning, and the cutting edge move of the Holy Spirit started there. Later, Antioch became the center of the revival. From there it spread to Constantinople, to Alexandria, and then to Rome.

After the apostasies of the Middle Ages, revival moved through Germany and other parts of Europe. Finally, it made its way to the Americas, and then to Asia and Africa. In our day, the Holy Spirit is now moving, but in a reverse course. Revival is returning to the place where it started, and it will soon be seen in the streets of Jerusalem once again.

The early Church began with apostles, and then there were prophets, evangelists, teachers and pastors. Now, again, these ministries are being restored in reverse order. We have rediscovered the role of the evangelist only in the past hundred years. At first, it was unheard of for someone to call himself an evangelist. Only pastors and teachers were acceptable.

Now the prophetic ministry is taking hold. The office and gifting of the prophet is more and more accepted. The final ministry to be restored will be that of apostle, and apostles are already recognized in some circles.

After the apostolic revival began in Jerusalem, Antioch became the center of it. Recently, a one-hundred-year-old building that formerly housed the French Embassy there was purchased by Pastor Kim Sundo of Kwang Lim Church. The building was purchased in order to plant a thoroughly modern Christian church in the city, along with a seminary. It will soon become a missionary-sending center, and missionaries will go out from Antioch in our time, just as they did in the days of Paul and Barnabas. When the apostolic ministry is fully restored, however, Jerusalem will be the center of revival and leadership for the Body of believers around the world. The center of the apostolic revival will have returned to the place of its birth.

We are living in the most exciting days in all of history. We are the generation that the apostles and prophets of old longed to see. In our day, the mysteries of the glory of God are being unveiled before us, and we can look forward to the imminent fulfillment of the Lord's promise:

> *"The earth will be filled with the knowledge of the glory of the Lord as the waters cover the sea."*

Epilogue

What God has begun will only intensify in the near future, and we will see more new and unusual signs of His glory. Recently, we have seen silver fillings changing to gold, and old, darkened fillings turning to silver. Isaiah prophesied:

> *"Instead of bronze I will bring gold,*
> *Instead of iron I will bring silver,*
> *Instead of wood, bronze,*
> *And instead of stones, iron."*   Isaiah 60:17

On our most recent trip to Chicago, some most unusual things happened. While many of the same miracles occurred — many healings (including cancer), multicolored dust on the walls and on the people, and gold and silver fillings and crowns in the shape of crosses and doves — there was something distinctly new. Angel feathers began to appear in the services.

The first time I heard about this manifestation was when Ruth Heflin told me that it had happened in the camp in Virginia. Then, several days later, someone showed me a feather that had appeared in this way. Since God was doing a new thing for others, I asked Him to do it for me too. And He did.

As I ministered in Chicago, the feathers miraculously began to appear all over the church — on the floor and on the seats. People kept coming forward during the meeting showing me more feathers that had manifested. We ended up with a bag full of them each night.

One lady said she had opened her front door that day, only to find "a whole mess" of feathers lying on her front porch. She didn't know what they were. When she came to the meeting that night, she realized that her feathers were the same as these that had fallen from Heaven. Others who attended had them appear "all over the place."

The very next day the pastor of that church shared in another church, and feathers also appeared there. These signs are contagious, and just testifying about them seems to bring them back.

On a Navajo Indian reservation in Ganado, Arizona, feathers also appeared in our meetings. The Native Americans know feathers, and they had an expert examine them. He said he had never seen a feather like that before.

I am convinced that these feathers are just one more sign that the glory of God and the presence of His holy angels is with us.

Each sign brings with it new revelation, insight

and direction. Feathers are from wings, and wings signify flight. This leads me to believe that the next thing we should expect is supernatural transportation, being taken to and from the heavens and to and fro upon the Earth.

Wings and flight also speak to us of a supernatural acceleration. What formerly took years to accomplish for God will now take us only a fraction of the time. We are now working with angelic help and God's speed.

Gold dust, gold teeth, angelic feathers, being transported in the Spirit ... this is only the beginning. God has many surprises in store for us in the near future, and we continue to believe for the *Mysteries of the Glory Unveiled.*

"For the earth will be filled
With the knowledge of the glory of the LORD,
As the waters cover the sea."

Habakkuk 2:14

— Notes —

— Notes —

— Notes —

— **Notes** —

— Notes —

— Notes —

Another great title by David Herzog:

Desperate

for

New

Wine

To order your copy, send a check or money order for $13.00 to the U.S. address on the following page. For those in Europe, send a Eurocheck to the French address (available also in French and Spanish).

Ministry Address

To contact David Herzog for crusades, conferences or revival meetings, or to receive more information about his ministry, please use one of the following addresses:

E-mail: daveherzog@aol.com
Visit our web site: voiceofglory.org

In the United States:

David Herzog
Revival Fire Ministries Intl.
325 Price Road #6
Sedona, AZ 86336
Fax: (214) 374-4485

In Europe:

David Herzog c/o A.C.B.B.
215, Ave. du Président Wilson,
93210 St. Denis
France
Fax: 01-49-17-11-25

* For those interested in receiving David Herzog's prayer/ partner letter, please send your name and address.